On Earth As It

The Letters in Red

A Study on the Words of Jesus

LEE WILKERSON

On Earth As It is in Heaven

The Letters in Red: A study on the Words of Jesus

Copyright© 2013 Lee Wilkerson

www.thelettersinred.com

Distributed by Crawford and Lee LLC, Akron, Ohio

ISBN 978-0-9914664-0-5

Cover design by Raymond S McCarthy.

TABLE OF CONTENTS

INTRODUCTION

J ESUS IS THE CHRIST, THE Son of the Living God. Multitudes proclaim His lordship and deity, saying "Lord, Lord", yet not doing the things He said "Do". The words of His lips have long ceased to be a driving force in churches in the West. People like Ghandi have been inspired to move nations by the sheer power of the teachings and example recorded in the Gospels; yet among Christians who claim to adhere to the biblical record, the words of our Lord are almost exclusively relegated to Sunday school: teachings for children who are not quite old enough to know how the real world works.

On the other hand, there are other Christian groups that have used the Sermon on the Mount as an example of moral teaching, but there is little account taken by these people of the claims of Jesus- they regard Him strictly as a great teacher. They are almost embarrassed by His statements that He is the Light of the world, that He is the Son of God, "Before Abraham was born, I Am"- and many others. For them He is the Great Example.

That is well and good; but there is certainly no reason to go to church or Sunday school to learn about a great example; that can be done much more effectively and cheaply at home.

But the fact of the matter is that we are not worshipping an example, nor are we giving heed to myths and fables. If Jesus is the Son of the living God, then His words are not to be taken as example, but as revelation- not merely as stories for emulation, but a picture of how reality works.

Jesus, the Word, is the revelation of the Father. His words are not merely teachings about, but windows into, the Kingdom of Heaven. The Church must allow the teachings of Jesus to change her view of reality, rather than allow the world around her to bend her view of the truth. Her views are to be shaped and informed by the teachings of our Lord. Those teachings are to be the blueprints by which the Holy Spirit builds the Kingdom of God. The teachings of Jesus are the witness given to the Church of the operations of the Holy Spirit, and conversely, the Spirit leads us into all truth, reminding us of those things which Jesus has said. Having said that we will know true teachers by their fruits, He gave us the words from the Father so that we could judge the shepherds from the hirelings.

The purpose of this book is to lay out the importance of our Lord's teachings in their relation to the Spirit of God and in the functioning of the Church. We will focus primarily on the teachings in the Synoptic Gospels, but will not limit ourselves strictly to them. We are in sore need of the power of the Holy Spirit in the Church today; and if by any chance the teachings of our Lord were meant to be a part of the true life of the Church, then we must openly acknowledge their absence from the life of the Church, repent, and ask for divine help.

In the first part of our study we lay out heavenly witness: Jesus' divine nature, His divine upbringing, the witness of the Father, the witness of the Son, and the witness of the Holy Spirit to His words. We also look into the witness of the Old Testament as well as the New Testament, and a cursory look at the witness of Church history to Jesus' teachings.

In the second part we deal with the various facets of the teachings of our Lord as relates to life as we know it- church practice, the total distortion of Paul's teachings by the popular preaching of our day, the effect of dispensationalism, and so forth.

We are living in a day when organized religion is being supplanted by disorganized religion. In addition there are those who for various reasons have relegated Jesus' teachings to the background; dispensational teachings have sometimes placed them as related to the Jews, to the future, or to the past. The simplistic doctrines of our day: "Jesus took care of all sin so we do not have to think about sin anymore, and he took care of righteousness so we don't have to think about that either" are becoming more front and center. There is a lot of activity but not much is accomplished. For multitudes the only thing in their theology is taking the next train out. It remains to be seen what will happen to the faith of multitudes when these self-serving theologies fall to the ground, but in any case, there are many views of the Bible, and many scenarios that people are clinging to.

In the midst of all of this stands the truth, and it comes with its witness

For the Law was given through Moses; grace and truth were realized through Jesus Christ. (Jn 1:17)

They were **realized through Jesus** in His obedience to the Father, just as they are realized in the Church in Her obedience to the Son. Grace will never operate without truth, and truth will be dead letter without grace.

Our prayer is not for the advancement of personal doctrine, but for the indwelling of the Spirit in the believer and the Church. God's presence only comes to fullness as the Spirit operates in the daily lives of believers as they share those things they have seen and heard from Him. As the Church is built up there comes a true witness to the grace of God, and not a witness that is built on human efforts.

When our Lord walked this earth He was faced with temptation. He was faced with people in a land torn by dissension, indignation over the evils of the day, questions about what the response to those evils should be: whether to bend to them, resist them, strike out on anger. . . In short, the problems of mankind and the quandary over what to do about them were just as real in His day as they are in ours. Our Lord experienced life as a man. He struggled to find the will of the Father, just like we do, and then He spoke. He did not speak out of His own reactions, but He spoke as the Father moved within Him. He spoke as One who saw and grasped everything- including the presence of the Father- in every situation. He saw our dilemmas and He saw the Father all at the same time. Having seen everything and having been publicly manifested as the Son of God by the Father, He opened His mouth and He taught them, saying. . .

But who was listening? Or rather, who is listening? Are we convinced that those words are more to be followed than the Declaration of Independence, or the even more venerated Bill of Rights? Just who are we listening to these days, anyway?

This little study certainly cannot tell you who you are listening to, only the power of God can do that; but we will certainly endeavor to explain who we should be listening to, and the consequences of not being guided by His teachings.

The church is powerless today for one reason: she has forsaken the way of life laid out for her by our Lord, and she has followed a course based on a partial reading of scripture. We must go back to the whole counsel of God. Until we do, our blessings will be scattered, not constant; the power of God in our midst will be hit or miss; our impact on society will be that of any other special interest group.

When God's people begin to live and think biblically, then out of the quietness of faithful lives God will speak. It will be a voice of transformation. It will be a voice of union, joining believers together in Christ. One thing is certain: God will not be with any people who have forsaken Him for another set of values. If the Church will keep His words, He will come to Her, and He will not come alone. The church is weak because she has left the One with the words of eternal life.

It's time to examine our ways.

PART 1

AS IT IS IN HEAVEN

1

JESUS: THE WORD OF GOD

"Jesus."

What more could God say?

God, after He spoke long ago to the fathers in the prophets in many portions and in many ways, in these last days has spoken to us in His Son, whom He appointed heir of all things, through whom also He made the world. (Heb 1:1-2)

Jesus is God's statement to fallen man. In Jesus, God declared Himself not just as being merciful, not just as being desirous of our salvation, not just as being the greatest Being in the universe, but in Jesus the true extent of that mercy, the full scope of that salvation and the very nature of that greatness are plainly revealed. **For in Him all the fullness of Deity dwells in bodily form (Col 2:9).**

Who is this Jesus?

The Bible reveals Him as the *Logos* of God: the very word of God. The Greek scholars tell us that the word *Logos* is more of a thought, a statement, or a declaration than it is a "word" in the modern sense. God did not send us a noun or a verb. He did not send us an adjective or even an interjection- even though modern man might like to think of Jesus as a short little irrelevant interlude in the affairs of history. No, God sent us a complete statement of Himself, all wrapped up in the Babe of Bethlehem; hidden, yet openly revealed to the world in the Miracle Worker; bathed in invisible glory on Golgotha; displayed to the eyes of faith in the resurrection of Jesus Christ from the dead; now available through the grace of God to all who seek Him.

Jesus.

Isn't He sufficient? What more could God say than to you He hath said? We certainly don't honor God by asking for an encore. We dare not insult God by asking, "What's next?" We receive Jesus knowing that He is the Father's ongoing proclamation of Himself.

In the beginning was the Word, and the Word was with God, and the Word was God. He was in the beginning with God. All things came into being through Him, and apart from Him nothing came into being that has come into being. In Him was life, and the life was the Light of men. (John 1:1-4)

God's statement of Himself was made of the same substance as He Himself. God was not revealing Himself to the world through an inferior being, but through One who was very God of very God. God did not entrust His revelation of Himself to a mere creation, but to the Creator Himself.

For by Him all things were created, both in the heavens and on earth, visible and invisible, whether thrones or dominions or

rulers or authorities- all things have been created through Him and for Him. (Col 1:16)

He was the One who could do a large labor and have the Father say of His work, "It is good." He could, in union with the Father, create man in the image and likeness of God, so much so that the breath of life could be breathed into man. This Creator was our Lord, the Word of God, the Son of God, the Lamb of God: Jesus.

And I saw heaven opened, and behold, a white horse, and He who sat on it is called Faithful and True, and in righteousness He judges and wages war. His eyes are a flame of fire, and on His head are many diadems; and He has a name written on Him which no one knows except Himself. He is clothed with a robe dipped in blood, and His name is called The Word of God. (Rev 19:11-13)

Even as the history of the word began with the STATEMENT of God producing a universe that the Father could take pleasure in, we see in the book of Revelation that near the end of human history that same STATEMENT is going to come with the armies of heaven to cleanse the earth. He will cleanse it in faithfulness, truth and righteousness: some of the very attributes that He shares with the Father. In Isaiah we see the immense glory of Jesus Christ

For a child will be born to us, a son will be given to us;

And the government will rest on His shoulders;

And His name will be called Wonderful Counselor, Mighty God,

Eternal Father, Prince of Peace.

There will be no end to the increase of His government or of peace,

On the throne of David and over his kingdom,

5

To establish it and to uphold it with justice and righteousness
From then on and forevermore.
The zeal of the LORD of hosts will accomplish this.
(Is 9:6&7)

"Jesus"

What more could God say? **Wonderful Counselor. Mighty
God. Eternal Father. Prince of Peace.** The Old Testament
plainly declares Him. No indication that the Father is jealous.
The only thing Jesus lacks in this passage is the throne of the
Father. In the book of Revelation (and in Daniel 7) we see that
the Father has given Him that as well.

**Then he showed me a river of the water of life, clear as
crystal, coming from the throne of God and of the Lamb,. . . . .
There will no longer be any curse; and the throne of God and
of the Lamb will be in it, and His bond-servants will serve Him;**
(Rev 22:1&3)

God and the Lamb: they share one throne. God and the
lamb: they share a life together. God and the Lamb: worshipped
together by the hosts of heaven. God and the Lamb: let's join
in worshipping them.

How did the Lamb get here? The book of Revelation describes it at length:

**Immediately I was in the Spirit; and behold, a throne was
standing in heaven, and One sitting on the throne. And He who
was sitting was like a jasper stone and a sardius in appearance;
and there was a rainbow around the throne, like an emerald in
appearance. (Rev 4:2-3)**

Here we see God upon His throne in the Holy of Holies.

**"Worthy are You, our Lord and our God, to receive glory and
honor and power; for You created all things, and because of Your
will they existed, and were created." (Rev 4:11)**

6

The Father receives adoration from the hosts of heaven. He who has all things, He who spoke and all things were created, He who cannot be increased by anything, is yet worthy to receive. Sure He is worthy to receive, but who can give Him anything? What meaning does all this adoration have for the Omnipotent? Can He even care what we think?

And I saw between the throne (with the four living creatures) and the elders a Lamb standing, as if slain, having seven horns and seven eyes, which are the seven Spirits of God, sent out into all the earth. And He came and took the book out of the right hand of Him who sat on the throne. When He had taken the book, the four living creatures and the twenty-four elders fell down before the Lamb, each one holding a harp and golden bowls full of incense, which are the prayers of the saints. And they sang a new song, saying, "Worthy are You to take the book and to break its seals; for You were slain, and purchased for God with Your blood men from every tribe and tongue and people and nation. "You have made them to be a kingdom and priests to our God; and they will reign upon the earth." Then I looked, and I heard the voice of many angels around the throne and the living creatures and the elders; and the number of them was myriads of myriads, and thousands of thousands, saying with a loud voice, "Worthy is the Lamb that was slain to receive power and riches and wisdom and might and honor and glory and blessing." And every created thing which is in heaven and on the earth and under the earth and on the sea, and all things in them, I heard saying, "To Him who sits on the throne, and to the Lamb, be blessing and honor and glory and dominion forever and ever." And the four living creatures kept saying, "Amen." And the elders fell down and worshiped. (Rev 5:6-14)

No doubt about whom the heavenly hosts think the Lamb is, there can be no doubt because He receives the same adoration as the Father. He can go up to the throne and take the book from the hand of Him Who Sits on the Throne. He is glorified by the heavenly hosts in the same breath as they glorify the Father. In this passage we have a clearer testimony to His lordship and deity than any theologian can give.

Jesus.

In Him we know that God cares. In Him we know that God wanted this earth to be just like it is in heaven. In Jesus was God's statement of what He desired to bring forth.

He who is worthy to be worshipped is worthy to be heard; He who takes the book becomes the custodian of it and the guardian of its contents. He who receives the full focus of the heavenly hosts' praise is certainly worthy of our undivided attention. In Jesus we have the only Being who is at home with the Father and with us.

He is the image of the invisible God, the firstborn of all creation. For by Him all things were created, both in the heavens and on earth, visible and invisible, whether thrones or dominions or rulers or authorities- all things have been created through Him and for Him. He is before all things, and in Him all things hold together. (Col 1:15-17)

"The image of the invisible God": this likeness, or image, is not an idolatrous image like a block of wood fashioned by a heathen trying to picture the divine features, but rather the living expression of God. Just as we see family resemblances between children and parents, brothers and sisters, so the divine countenance is revealed in the face of Jesus Christ. The Father and the Son are obviously related; all can see the same essence in the Father and the Son. He is a true Son, pictured in Revelation 5 receiving His inheritance from the Father. Because of this likeness He can create the universe in the name of the

Father, according to the Father's specifications. Because of this common DNA that He shares with the Father, He can govern according to the heart of the Father. Because of His person as the Word of God, He can speak the words of the Father in purity.

The words of the LORD are pure words;

As silver tried in a furnace on the earth, refined seven times. (Ps 12:6)

While on the earth He showed forth the Father-

Jesus *said to him, "Have I been so long with you, and yet you have not come to know Me, Philip? He who has seen Me has seen the Father; how can you say, 'Show us the Father'?" (Jn 14:9)

Jesus came to declare the Father. The Jews of Jesus' day were looking for the Messiah; they wanted a healer, they wanted a savior, they wanted somebody who would beat the daylights out of the Romans. They just didn't want a revelation of the Father; such a thing was foreign to their thinking, alien to their hearts, and contrary to centuries of accumulated scholarly ignorance.

Jesus's open portrayal of the Father went against both their expectations and their interests. The Jews wanted God on a throne, overwhelming the senses. They wanted God in majesty and splendor. They wanted God, well, yes, to be worshipped, but not requiring any other mundane human responses-certainly not God revealing Himself with a Galilean accent. In any case the Jews were certain that God could not be revealed in the flesh. They were certain that all was revealed in the Law (which they did not understand for the same reason) and that the only thing that was yet to be done was to set up a political kingdom. They were certain that God would swoop down from heaven with a big army, defeat the powers of this world, and it would be every man under his vine and his fig tree, much the same way as the churches today present the purposes of God. There was nothing in any of this with enough skin on it to challenge any of the daily assumptions of life, or to form and shape a people who would worship God and be His peculiar people, which was God's purpose in taking Israel out of Egypt, and His purpose in taking us out of sin.

They were enamored of the grand, the glorious, and the future, and so they missed their Messiah, just like most Christians have missed their Messiah: great expectations, but a resolute refusal to truly perceive the Man of Sorrows. Jesus the Savior, yes, but not allowed- at least by most- to be the revealer of the Father. Divine, yes; the second person of the Trinity, yes; the Church has that part of the theology right- anything that does not affect 'life on planet Earth'. But as for His being the Word of God- the One who reveals the Father- they would regard this as possible only as a theological concept or an eschatological hope. God revealed Himself in Jesus in the last dispensation, and will reveal Himself in the next dispensation, but they are not expecting anything in this life that will affect their lifestyles, their routines, or their expenditures. They worship Him as he who was, and is not, and is to come, and not as the Great I AM.

There is a branch of Christianity for whom Jesus is the great Teacher, the great Moralist. They honor Him as the proclaimer of the highest ethical system the world has ever seen; His teachings being perfectly rational- perhaps a bit idealistic- but largely understandable to the average person. They would emphasize the social good that such teachings do, the positive effects on society, the help for the poor, the alleviation of poverty, etc., etc., etc.

That was not the way He wanted to be known, and that view is not what this book is expressing. Jesus did not come to earth, go to the cross, rise from the dead, and fill His followers with the Holy Spirit in order to lay out principles for dead flesh to try to execute. Turning Jesus' teachings into social ideals - or any other kind of ideals for that matter - does not elevate Him to a high enough level to allow Him to get into the heart and produce the new kind of person who can actually do anything about these teachings. He wants to get inside us so that we can know Him as one knows one's own thoughts.

So part of the Christian world worships Him idolatrously- as God and God alone, though giving lip service to His human nature, and another part of the Christian world pays heed to His teachings, but not enough to His person to allow His living presence to have any practical effect in changing the heart.

Jesus came because the Father had something to say and He wanted it said as clearly as possible. What He wanted to say was about Himself in plain language that even (or only!) a child could understand.

God, after He spoke long ago to the fathers in the prophets in many portions and in many ways, in these last days has spoken to us in His Son, whom He appointed heir of all things, through whom also He made the world. And He is the radiance of His glory and the exact representation of His nature, and upholds all things by the word of His power. When He had made purification of sins, He sat down at the right hand of the Majesty on high, having become as much better than the angels, as He has inherited a more excellent name than they. (Heb 1:1-3)

The Son is God's proclamation. God spoke in the Old Testament in a variety of ways. Some of the prophets went through horrible personal situations because God wanted them

11

to be living embodiments of His message to Israel. Ezekiel's wife died and he was not allowed to mourn. Isaiah had to give strange names to his children. Hosea had to marry a faithless woman and then throw away good money after bad in buying her back out of servitude. The prophets were living examples of God's message to Israel. In these days God speaks to us in Jesus, and God means what He says. The Son is not a symbol; He is the full expression of the Father.

Only a son can truly know a father. He receives the personal interest and training from the father. Internally he has the DNA of the father, which is the internal likeness, and externally he is shaped by the father's hand.

In the same way Jesus the Son is not just a distant representative of the Father, but a living expression of the Father, and of the household of the Father. He grew up in the Father's house, which was the living outworking of the Father's view of life. God sent the only One who could not only tell us about the Father, but who could also get the Father's servants here on earth into line with the ways of the Father's servants in heaven. He was telling the truth when He said, "I must be about My Father's business." Only the Son could receive the instructions on how to get the creation back into the proper order. He chose, by the Father's orders, to die instead.

That tells us something, and what it tells us is deeply indicative of the heart of the Father.

Look again at Colossians 1:

He is the image of the invisible God, the firstborn of all creation. For by Him all things were created, both in the heavens and on earth, visible and invisible, whether thrones or dominions or rulers or authorities- all things have been created through Him and for Him. He is before all things, and in Him all things hold

together. He is also head of the body, the church; and He is the beginning, the firstborn from the dead, so that He Himself will come to have first place in everything. (Col 1:15-18)

Consider the idea of the 'firstborn.' In the Old Testament the firstborn of the flocks or herds was totally dedicated to the Lord. The firstborn was the sacrificial animal. In saying that Jesus was the 'firstborn of all creation', the Bible was saying that He was totally dedicated to the Lord. He was not His own. He was to be offered up. If He had come as a firstborn king, maybe He would have taken over everything. Inasmuch as He was the Lamb of God, He was born to die. Rather than choose preeminence, He took the lowest place,

who, although He existed in the form of God, did not regard equality with God a thing to be grasped, but emptied Himself, taking the form of a bond-servant, and being made in the likeness of men. Being found in appearance as a man, He humbled Himself by becoming obedient to the point of death, even death on a cross. For this reason also, God highly exalted Him, and bestowed on Him the name which is above every name, so that at the name of Jesus EVERY KNEE WILL BOW, of those who are in heaven and on earth and under the earth, and that every tongue will confess that Jesus Christ is Lord, to the glory of God the Father. (Php 2:6-11)

He has received the Name. Not the "a name" of the King James Version, but the Name which was too sacred to even pronounce. The Name that was revealed to Moses as just simply "I AM" was bequeathed upon Jesus by the only One who could confer that holiest of names.

This firstborn Son received the inheritance not through the death of His Father, but by dying and surrendering all claim to anything except the sheer mercy of the Father. This

Firstborn Son didn't move by human rules because He was revealing the laws of heaven. God was being unveiled in Jesus by His life, by His words, by His death, by His burial, by His resurrection, and by His ascension. Men could not figure out any of this.

In many cultures the firstborn son is accorded a special place: he will inherit the family business or property, and become the head of the family. In return, he will take care of the father and mother in their old age. Because the firstborn will carry on the family name, he gets special training from the father as well as special responsibilities. Many of the highest executives in Japan are firstborn sons. They received a rougher upbringing than their younger siblings and were trained from childhood to take responsibility. They were not allowed to get away with anything. They learned to be decisive, to take charge and lead.

Therefore, holy brethren, partakers of a heavenly calling, consider Jesus, the Apostle and High Priest of our confession; He was faithful to Him who appointed Him, as Moses also was in all His house. For He has been counted worthy of more glory than Moses, by just so much as the builder of the house has more honor than the house. For every house is built by someone, but the builder of all things is God. Now Moses was faithful in all His house as a servant, for a testimony of those things which were to be spoken later; but Christ was faithful as a Son over His house whose house we are, if we hold fast our confidence and the boast of our hope firm until the end. (Heb 3:1-6)

So we see a faithful Son, faithful and able to move in the nature of the Father. He was not just faithful in an abstract sort of way, but He was faithful to the Father in the midst of the household- He could put things in order and God would say, "Well done."

14

Of course, since He is the offspring of the Father, He shares the same genetic material as the Father: the family characteristics are carried on. The Son is the product of the Father's genes as well as the product of His hands; He is both begotten and molded by the Father. He was capable both by nature and training to carry on the name of the Father in the earth.

The Bible tells us that Jesus is the Word. That means little to modern man: talk is cheap. To proclaim to 20th- century man that Jesus is the Word may sound more like God's advertising program than something worthy of serious consideration. Certainly there is little in our culture to inspire awe in our souls at the thought of the "Word of God." In fact there is little in our society or our churches to bring us to a reverent fear of much of anything to do with God. Even elevating God above the common is somewhat foreign to our thinking. God is our friend (which is true). God loves us (which is certainly true). God knows us and wants us to know Him; and yet He came unto His own and His own received Him not. If we knew the gift of God and who it was that was speaking. . .

And so the unknown God speaks to us today through a Son.

Jesus is *the Logos*. That does not make Him a grammatical unit composed of letters. It does not mean that He is a Word like other words, only better; it means that He is the message, the very content of the heart of God opened up before mankind.

If the Father is speaking to us through a Son, what is He saying?

"And He is the radiance of His glory and the exact representation of His nature," (Heb 1:3a)

What could He say but that which was from the Father?

15

In the Old Testament, God spoke in bits and pieces. He spoke through rituals and prophets and wars and poetry. Now He speaks with clarity in His Son. Before, there were veiled references; now there is open declaration: "**He who has seen me has seen the Father.**"(Jn14:9b) How could we not reckon that "He that has heard me has heard the Father?"

Jesus is the declaration of the Father to the creation. He is not only the Word of the Father, but He is the accurate expression of the Father to the creation.

No one has seen God at any time; the only begotten God who is in the bosom of the Father, He has explained Him. (John 1:18).

Jesus is "**In the bosom of the Father.**" What was He doing there? What could have been placed in Him through being the "**only begotten God, which is in the bosom of the Father?**"

Only the knowledge that comes through intimate fellowship with the Father.

Jesus was in the bosom of the Father because the Father had something to say and He wanted Jesus to say it.

"**This is My beloved Son: listen to Him!**" (Mk 9:7b)

We will now look at how the man Jesus was taught by the Father.

2

A Faithful Son Learns

THEREFORE JESUS ANSWERED AND WAS saying to them, "Truly, truly, I say to you, the Son can do nothing of Himself, unless it is something He sees the Father doing; for whatever the Father does, these things the Son also does in like manner. For the Father loves the Son, and shows Him all things that He Himself is doing; and the Father will show Him greater works than these, so that you will marvel." (John 5:19&20)

In heavenly things, the sons of Adam have to rely on other eyes. Mortal creatures that we are, there is no way that we can know the things of God. Since God's ways are far above our ways, He must reach down and communicate with us. God's kingdom is totally foreign to our nature: it is not intuitive, it is not even analogous. It is reached neither by the intellect nor the will. Man failed to get there physically at the Tower of

Babel. Flesh and blood cannot see the Kingdom of God; God had to bridge the gap between heaven and earth, and He did.

Since man was by nature incapable of reaching out to God, the Father Himself moved on our behalf. He sent Jesus, the Mediator who bridged the gap; Jesus, the Word incarnate; Jesus, full of grace and truth; Jesus, who has declared the Father. He did not come in splendor, He did not come as the reigning king; He came to a stable in Bethlehem. He came to shepherds and foreign wise men, to commoners. He came to experience human life from the bottom up.

As man He could experience the compassion of the Father. He saw its full scope. He became as a little child. Yes, He became a child in the manger in Bethlehem, but He also became a child in the things of His Father. He came as One with no intuition about what He had been. He had to start all over again from square one; so, as an obedient Child He accepted the limits imposed on Him by the Father and received the instruction of the Father, just as we must.

Small wonder that He tells us to become as little children. Small wonder that He wants us reduced to absolute dependence. Small wonder that it is easier to believe that He is the Son of God 'way back when and way up there' than to pay attention to what He has said, just as many people acknowledge their fathers even if they don't heed what they say. His words run contrary to fallen man, just as the words of a father run contrary to the desires and instincts of a little child, yet the child's life depends on absorbing the word of the parents.

Jesus came in the most absurd role in history: apparently illegitimate, poor, from a backward area in Palestine, to preach a message that could not be understood by anyone who would hear Him.

but Christ was faithful as a Son over His house- whose house we are, if we hold fast our confidence and the boast of our hope firm until the end. (Heb 3:6)

He, the unlimited, accepted limits- our limits: to possess only what He was given; to be misunderstood; to be framed in not only by a body, but by a soul; to be faced with command-ments He would rather not do, just as with us. We can only expect to receive instruction on the Kingdom of God from One who has experienced the Father as Teacher. The Master was, Himself, a student.

One thing He had that we don't: since He was the Son, it was given Him to know the Father. This He received by birth: we receive this only by new birth. Once we have that birth we are adopted into the family and receive the instruction con-cerning the family we've been born into, even as He received instruction from the Father.

And He said to them, "Why is it that you were looking for Me? Did you not know that I had to be in My Father's {1} house?" {1) Or affairs; lit in the things of My Father? (Luke 2:49)

The Son was in the things of My Father. And so He was brought up to do what pleased the Father. At this point, at twelve years of age, He reached full realization of who He was, and who His Father was. From this point on, more and more, He was in communion with His Father.

And Jesus kept increasing in wisdom and stature, and in favor with God and men. (Luke 2:52)

God was pleased: the Son had the revelation of His Father. He was going to be listening only to Him from this point on.

19

The Son Hears and Sees the Father

Jesus had access to the Father. He was not just a distant correspondent to represent the Father's interests in a faraway land-He was in vital touch with the Father as He taught, as He performed miracles, and as He went on His journeys. Without the Father He was nothing. When He emptied Himself (Php 2:6-8), He reduced Himself to absolute dependence on the Father; being found in fashion as a man, He humbled Himself even to death on a cross- the one thing He would have to go through totally alone.

The Son communed with the Father for His very life: in the same way we are to commune with the Son for our life. The Son refused to run on His own steam: therefore we are not to run on our own steam, but to rely on the Son.

"As the living Father sent Me, and I live because of the Father, so he who eats Me, he also will live because of Me. This is the bread which came down out of heaven; not as the fathers ate and died; he who eats this bread will live forever." (Jn 6:57)

So Jesus said, "When you lift up the Son of Man, then you will know that I am He, and I do nothing on My own initiative, but I speak these things as the Father taught Me." (Jn 8:28)

Why was the creator of the universe taught? Why did He who is called the Wisdom of God receive instruction? Because the Captain of our salvation was bringing many sons to glory, and He Himself was showing the way. He, by learning, was showing that all who are His must learn.

Therefore Jesus answered and was saying to them, "Truly, truly, I say to you, the Son can do nothing of Himself, unless it is something He sees the Father doing; for whatever the Father does, these things the Son also does in like manner. For the Father loves

the Son, and shows Him all things that He Himself is doing; and the Father will show Him greater works than these, so that you will marvel." (John 5:19&20)

"I can do nothing on My own initiative. As I hear, I judge; and My judgment is just, because I do not seek My own will, but the will of Him who sent Me." (John 5:30)

Jesus, by these words states categorically that He, who was the freest of men, was not functioning as a free agent. He was not doing His own thing. He was not bound by the 21st century definition of freedom. When He said, "The Son can do nothing of Himself", He was saying that, having shared in the glory of the Eternal Father, and being omnipotent Himself, He had used His omnipotence to lay aside omnipotence and be fashioned as a man. He was still the Son. He was still the second person of the Trinity, but without form or comeliness, without majesty or splendor, in weakness rather than strength: God, reduced to a root out of dry ground, reduced to obedience, reduced to complete dependence. Although He could have called 10,000 angels because of Who He was in Himself and the authority yet resident within Him, He cried out in despair because of who He was in His submission to His God- appointed station in life.

Deity is not easy.

The omnipotent Son reduced Himself to, "Yes Father."

As a man speaking to men, as the divine Son hearing from the Father; as the One whom God sent, He made known to us the very heart of God in the words that He spoke. These were the commandments of the Father to a special Son.; words that only He could hear; words that the disciples could not understand then; words that required the coming of the Holy Spirit before they could take root in the hearts of men. We know them as the letters in red.

The delivery of these words was the one thing the Father told the Son to do before Calvary.

"For I did not speak on My own initiative, but the Father Himself who sent Me has given Me a commandment as to what to say and what to speak. I know that His commandment is eternal life; therefore the things I speak, I speak just as the Father has told Me." (Jn 12:49)

for the words which You gave Me I have given to them; and they received them and truly understood that I came forth from You, and they believed that You sent Me. (Jn 17:8)

Jesus would leave the needy crowds in order to slip away into the desert and teach His disciples. The compassion in Him was struggling with the commandment of the Father to impart the word to the disciples. The words that He spoke to them came from His abiding relationship with the Father, and were evidence thereof. They were the power of the Father working in the Son.

"Do you not believe that I am in the Father, and the Father is in Me? The words that I say to you I do not speak on My own initiative, but the Father abiding in Me does His works." (Jn 14:10)

We will have more on this verse later, but suffice it to say that the words which He spoke were the very outflow of the presence of the Father, showing in words the things transpiring not only in heaven, but in God Himself.

"I speak the things which I have seen with My Father; therefore you also do the things which you heard from your father." (John 8:38)

The words which Jesus spoke were the things that He, as the perfect Son, was seeing and hearing from the Father. He was seeing things that we don't have access to. He was hearing

22

the most important words that there have ever been. He was being shown, as a man, the things that were His domain before the world began. Heaven was being opened up to Him, and then He opened His mouth and taught them saying. . . . .

3

THE WORDS OF JESUS AND THE FATHER

The Father: the Source of the Words of Jesus

"But I tell you that every careless word that people speak, they shall give an accounting for it in the day of judgment." (Mt 12:36)

Careless words - what a description of the world today. It will be a long, slow line on Judgment Day when God takes a reckoning of every careless word. Our tongues pour forth the careless, the useless and the banal. Our televisions go for hours with careless words. Politicians get elected with glib promises. One of the prime characteristics of the world today is careless words.

Mankind is uniquely qualified to pour out meaningless speech because mankind is somewhat schizophrenic: a blend of contrarieties all bundled up in one package. Within each person are desires, aspirations and wants, yet even our desires are at cross purposes: we want to eat our cake and lose weight at the same time. We want to reduce the amount of stuff cluttering up our homes, but we don't want to get rid of anything. We want to serve God without it costing anything.

By nature we are living, breathing, contradictions.

This internal division was the result of the fall of man. Before the fall, Adam was at one with God, the woman, and the earth. When man ate from the tree of the knowledge of good and evil, then good and evil rattled around in the mind of man without communion with God to bring definition and clarification. Adam became separated from himself, from God, from the woman, and from the creation. All was struggle. Conflicts raging within the divided soul were made visible when Cain killed Abel. There was no peace within or without.

These divisions are all typical of our human predicament; they come from a divided inner man. James says:

What is the source of quarrels and conflicts among you? Is not the source your pleasures that wage war in your members? You lust and do not have; so you commit murder. You are envious and cannot obtain; so you fight and quarrel. You do not have because you do not ask. You ask and do not receive, because you ask with wrong motives, so that you may spend it on your pleasures. (James 4:1-3)

Again he says:

But if any of you lacks wisdom, let him ask of God, who gives to all generously and without reproach, and it will be given to him. But he must ask in faith without any doubting, for the one who doubts is like the surf of the sea, driven and tossed by the wind. For that man ought not to expect that he will receive anything from the Lord, being a double-minded man, unstable in all his ways. (James 1:5-8)

26

Even in his desire to serve God, the heart of man is devious; whether the religious elite that crucified the Lord Jesus, or the religious person out to build a bigger church - only God can weigh the motives. All these people work with the words of God as processed through the soul of man. After 2000 years of Church history, the church on earth is a living proof of the divided heart of man. Although God's purpose in Christ was to undo the damage done by the Fall, even here, when the Creator of all came, the fallen heart could not receive Him.

We were born into that broken condition, absolutely incapable of fellowship with God, hardly at peace with ourselves, totally fragmented.

God is not like this. The Bible proclaims His unity from the beginning to the end; **"Hear, O Israel! The LORD is our God, the LORD is one!"**(Dt 6:4) Even in the plurality of the Father, Son, and Holy Spirit, God is one. There is no strife between the Father and the Son. The Holy Spirit is not chafing for more recognition. When we behold the Son, we are beholding the undivided heart of the Father made manifest. We are receiving counsel that will never contradict or mislead when we listen to the Spirit of God. All comes together because it all came out of a unified heart, a perfect heart.

The mouth of the righteous is a fountain of life,

But the mouth of the wicked conceals violence. (Pro 10:11)

God speaks out of the unity of His Being; therefore His words give life. Man speaks out of the disunity of his being, therefore man's words tend to conceal. God speaks from a pure heart; man has no pure heart- only God can produce that. Man must fight hypocrisy. Man must resist being devious. Children do not need lessons in how to lie, just as adults don't need encouragement to fudge on their income taxes. We were born

27

in sin and only by the grace of God do we find escape from its clutches.

God lives above this realm.

The words of the LORD are pure words;

As silver tried in a furnace on the earth, refined seven times. (Ps 12:6)

These words come, as all words do, from the abundance of the heart, but they come from a heart that reveals. They come as the unveiling of the Speaker. They show us the thoughts of God- not a carefully studied campaign speech that focuses on putting forward an appealing face. They are not just His thoughts, but His very heart.

"You brood of vipers, how can you, being evil, speak what is good? For the mouth speaks out of that which fills the heart. The good man brings out of his good treasure what is good; and the evil man brings out of his evil treasure what is evil." (Mt 12:34&35)

As with the good man, so with God- He speaks out of the overflow of His heart: pure words, words which reveal.

But He answered and said, "It is written, 'MAN SHALL NOT LIVE ON BREAD ALONE, BUT ON EVERY WORD THAT PROCEEDS OUT OF THE MOUTH OF GOD.'" (Mat 4:4)

From the fountain of life we receive words that give life. We live by those words, whether they came from God 4000 years ago or just yesterday, those words that He has spoken are our life.

"It is the Spirit who gives life; the flesh profits nothing; the words that I have spoken to you are spirit and are life." (Jn 6:63)

Jesus' words are more than good idea words, they are more than God's PR campaign; they are a fountain of life because they come from the heart of the Father and the Son.

"Do you not believe that I am in the Father, and the Father is in Me? The words that I say to you I do not speak on My own initiative, but the Father abiding in Me does His works. Believe Me that I am in the Father and the Father is in Me; otherwise believe because of the works themselves." (John 14:10&11)

At first glance verse 10 is a mystery: it talks about Jesus speaking and those words being related to the working of the Father. When Jesus spoke He didn't just report what He saw and heard, He opened His mouth and what came out was the sound of hammers and saws from the workshop of the Father. The words He was speaking were the sounds of the Father at work. Jesus was saying, "Blessed are the merciful." When we hear these words, generally we hear a radical idea that we somehow are supposed to fit into our lives. These words, however, are actually the sound of the Father being merciful to us, drawing us up into Himself if we will but embrace those words by faith and allow the Spirit of God to activate them, first in our renewed minds, then in our lives.

When Jesus spoke in Genesis 1, God was active: the Son spoke, and it was. That is how it was in the beginning of the first creation, and that is the pattern of the new creation: Jesus' words are not just grammatical entities, they are bundles of the power of God. His words are spirit and they are life. They are the very activity of the Father in the Son. Jesus was not speaking good ideas; He received His words from the Father. His words were not just teachings for man; they were fountains of life for man, by which we live. His words were the very working of the Father in the Son, revealing, giving life. Jesus' words are the very working of the Spirit in our lives, bringing us into that same image.

We read earlier that Jesus' words are spirit and life. They are not of this order of creation. Jesus Himself is the Word, and

His words express the essence of that life. His words are the dictionary by which all life is defined; they are active, living words, just as Father's words are.

For the word of God is living and active and sharper than any two-edged sword, and piercing as far as the division of soul and spirit, of both joints and marrow, and able to judge the thoughts and intentions of the heart. (Heb 4:12)

God's word is not just a sequence of ideas that He recommends for our consideration, they are the vital connection between us and the Spirit of God Who seeks to enact them in the heart of every believer.

for the words which You gave Me I have given to them; and they received them and truly understood that I came forth from You, and they believed that You sent Me. (John 17:8)

"For He whom God has sent speaks the words of God; for He gives the Spirit without measure." (John 3:34)

So Jesus answered them and said, "My teaching is not Mine, but His who sent Me. If anyone is willing to do His will, he will know of the teaching, whether it is of God or whether I speak from Myself." (John 7:16&17)

So Jesus said, "When you lift up the Son of Man, then you will know that I am He, and I do nothing on My own initiative, but I speak these things as the Father taught Me." (John 8:28)

"I speak the things which I have seen with My Father; therefore you also do the things which you heard from your father." (John 8:38)

There is no mistaking where He got those words He spoke when He was on earth: these were the words of the Father. They are the expression of what Jesus heard and saw from the Father in His time on earth. Because they were the word of the Father, they come from the abundance of His heart, the heart

30

of the Father. Because Jesus was the One who received them, He who was the very Word of God Himself, these words could be transmitted purely and truly.

We may all think we agree on this, but let's bring this down to earth.

When Jesus says, "**Blessed are the meek,**" then this is not just a nice idea. This is not just one perspective on reality. This is a statement from God that the Son received, because only He could receive something like this. Now, this was one of the words Jesus received from the Father not just to give us religious ideas, not just to lead us to speculation about what meekness might happen to mean. This is not an arbitrary saying that could have been otherwise, e.g. "Blessed are the powerful," because the All Powerful could not say this, because although He is omnipotent, such a statement about power is not in His heart. This is not just a nice ethical teaching about what we are supposed to be like; this is first and foremost a revelation of the heart of the Father. The meek are blessed because there is something in the heart of God that corresponds to meekness. This statement is revelatory of God in His being. Jesus is meek, therefore He is the Blessed One. Jesus is now rich, having dominion on earth and heaven. This, however, is not why He is blessed; He is blessed because He is poor in spirit, meek, He weeps, He has patience- go ahead and read Matthew 5:1-12. He was the Blessed One. He still is. These words that He spoke are still active, they are still a fountain of life, they are still the unveiling of the Father.

In the Sermon on the Mount Jesus told us about the Father. We thought He was talking about us and what we ought to do, or be, or at least want to do or be. . . . But let's look-

"**You have heard that it was said, 'YOU SHALL LOVE YOUR NEIGHBOR and hate your enemy.' But I say to you, love your** enemies and pray for those who persecute you, so that you may be sons of your Father who is in heaven; for He causes His sun to rise on the evil and the good, and sends rain on the righteous and the unrighteous. For if you love those who love you, what reward do you have? Do not even the tax collectors do the same? If you greet only your brothers, what more are you doing than others? Do not even the Gentiles do the same? Therefore you are to be perfect, as your heavenly Father is perfect." (Mt 5:43-48)

This passage can be viewed on one level as telling us what we ought to do. But, as with so many things in the Bible, there is more to it than just that. Verse 45 introduces the idea of being sons of the Father. So apparently we're supposed to do this so that we will become sons of the Father. So we are all to go out and try to love our neighbors. . . .

However, the central fact of this is that this is first and foremost how God is: He lets the sun shine on the wicked, and He lets the rain fall on the unjust. These commands are not to give us some more things to do, but first of all to teach us of our Father. They are not just ideas to teach our children, but these are active, fountain of life words that quicken our spirits because they are spirit words, words that illuminate the divine life: that life that was first in the Father and that was given to us at our new birth. These words describe the New Man.

Do not lie to one another, since you laid aside the old self with its evil practices, and have put on the new self who is being renewed to a true knowledge according to the image of the One who created him — a renewal in which there is no distinction between Greek and Jew, circumcised and uncircumcised, barbarian, Scythian, slave and freeman, but Christ is all, and in all.

So, as those who have been chosen of God, holy and beloved, put on a heart of compassion, kindness, humility, gentleness and

patience; bearing with one another, and forgiving each other, whoever has a complaint against anyone; just as the Lord forgave you, so also should you. Beyond all these things put on love, which is the perfect bond of unity. (Col 3:9-14)

Here we see the New Man and the whole thing is connected with the burying of distinction. It is coupled with compassion, kindness, humility, gentleness, patience, forbearance and forgiveness, and let's not forget love. Not hard to find all these characteristics in Jesus' teachings, but Paul is not going to talk about the new creation without drawing in these principles as well. All these things are of the new creation and all are out of the heart of the Father. (Notice the reference to "**after the image of him that created him.**")

If the Sermon on the Mount is just a series of good ideas for spiritual superstars, then I can applaud their heroics and go my way. If, however, this is how God is, then there will never be communion with the Father any other way. We will find that, far from being an ethical code, these words are an open statement of the heart that saved me, and these words also reveal the heart that was given to me when I was saved. I don't bless those that curse me simply because this is the higher way; I bless those that curse me because the Father does this, and as I find the Father, I find that heart that saved me, forgave me and now empowers me to show this life- His life- to the world.

The words of Jesus express the life that found me when I was in darkness, and God made his light to shine on a lost one (me!). This is the life that found me in sin and blessed me with the showers from heaven. The forgiveness we've found in God is the source of our power to forgive others. The voice that took me when I was under accusation and set me free is the voice that said "**I do not condemn you, either. Go. From now on sin** no more." (Jn 8:11b) And when I heard those words, they were meant to be a revelation of the power that was now resident within me to walk in newness of life and not in oldness of the letter. They were meant to cause me to present myself to God as one alive from the dead and my body as a weapon of righteousness. That power was inherent in the Spirit who now lives within, and that power is released as these words are mixed with faith. This is Jesus's doctrine and this is Paul's doctrine. (We will talk more about Paul later). The more we know the Father as revealed by Jesus' words, the more we have an idea of the scope of God's grace. Jesus gives us impossible commands, not to destroy us or set up an obstacle course, but to show the magnitude of His grace toward us who believe.

"Let your light shine before men in such a way that they may see your good works, and glorify your Father who is in heaven." (Mt 5:16)

If these are words the Father gave the Son that His life might be formed in us on this earth, then it is true that:

"Therefore everyone who hears these words of Mine and acts on them, may be compared to a wise man who built his house on the rock. And the rain fell, and the floods came, and the winds blew and slammed against that house; and yet it did not fall, for it had been founded on the rock. Everyone who hears these words of Mine and does not act on them, will be like a foolish man who built his house on the sand. The rain fell, and the floods came, and the winds blew and slammed against that house; and it fell — and great was its fall." (Mt 7:24-27)

Since this way of understanding truth is totally foreign to modern western man, let's look at a familiar parable, the Parable of the Good Samaritan to see how some of this works in practical life. As you read this parable your mind will be turned to the Samaritan, and how you ought to be like that. It will come through to most people as an object lesson to imitate- but that has nothing to do with the parable; it is given to answer the question, "Who is my neighbor?"

And a lawyer stood up and put Him to the test, saying, "Teacher, what shall I do to inherit eternal life?" And He said to him, "What is written in the Law? How does it read to you?" And he answered, "YOU SHALL LOVE THE LORD YOUR GOD WITH ALL YOUR HEART, AND WITH ALL YOUR SOUL, AND WITH ALL YOUR STRENGTH, AND WITH ALL YOUR MIND; AND YOUR NEIGHBOR AS YOURSELF." And He said to him, "You have answered correctly; DO THIS AND YOU WILL LIVE." But wishing to justify himself, he said to Jesus, "And who is my neighbor?" Jesus replied and said, "A man was going down from Jerusalem to Jericho, and fell among robbers, and they stripped him and beat him, and went away leaving him half dead. And by chance a priest was going down on that road, and when he saw him, he passed by on the other side. Likewise a Levite also, when he came to the place and saw him, passed by on the other side. But a Samaritan, who was on a journey, came upon him; and when he saw him, he felt compassion, and came to him and bandaged up his wounds, pouring oil and wine on them; and he put him on his own beast, and brought him to an inn and took care of him. On the next day he took out two denarii and gave them to the innkeeper and said, 'Take care of him; and whatever more you spend, when I return I will repay you.' Which of these three do you think proved to be a neighbor to the man who fell into the robbers' hands?" And he said, "The one who showed mercy toward him." Then Jesus said to him, "Go and do the same." (Lk 10:25-37)

Jesus was teaching and a question came: "Teacher, what shall I do to inherit eternal life?"

Jesus followed the safe path and asked him what the Book said. The lawyer even came up with the right answer - love God, love your neighbor. . . Not too heavy - been there done that. But ohh. . . who is my neighbor? Where is the line between who I have to love and who I don't have to love? This is the heart of fallen man, and this is where Jesus is going to speak a parable that leaves legalism far behind and leads us into the heart of the Father: there is no "who do I have to love" in the Kingdom.

We all know the parable, but almost no one has ever read the question Jesus asks at the end: **"Which of these three do you think proved to be a neighbor to the man who fell into the robbers' hands?"** He did not ask, "Who is the neighbor of the guy on the donkey?" He did not ask who the neighbor is of the healthy and the strong. He did not ask about the neighbor of the wealthy and well connected, any more than He asks about the neighbor of the smug and self- complacent. He does not care who the neighbor of these people is; I repeat: He Does Not Care. He wants us to tell Him who the neighbor of the guy on the ground is. Who is the neighbor of the one who is lost? Who is the neighbor of the fatherless and the widow? Who is the neighbor of the helpless?

We always want to know who our neighbor is as if we're riding fat and sassy, picking and choosing upon whom to rain our benevolence. Jesus does not have an answer to that question, and he never will. He asks us, "Who is the neighbor of the guy on the ground?" not, "Who is your neighbor now that things are prosperous and finances are OK and the family problems are under control."

In His answer to the lawyer's question, He only lets us identify with the guy on the ground - and who IS his neighbor?

Well, let's ask: who was my neighbor when I was beaten and bleeding? Who was my neighbor when the finances were tough, or the family was coming unglued, or the diagnosis was most hopeless.

Just who is my neighbor?

The One Who Showed Mercy

After a full recognition of who my Neighbor is, He says, **"Go and do likewise."**

(If this is still a mystery, if you are still wondering what you are supposed to do, read Romans 5:8 farther down.)

When we have seen that the One Who showed mercy is our neighbor, this puts it in a different light. No longer am I being asked to imitate a mythical Samaritan; I am being pointed to the Father, but not merely to imitate the abstract ethics of God Almighty, but rather to be like I found Him to be at the very point of contact - the point at which He poured in the oil and the wine; the point at which He bandaged me up; the point at which He paid the bill and offered to cover the other expenses: I meet Him at the point of His mercy. There it is that He says, **"Go, and do likewise."** Whether you are a billionaire or a pauper, there is only one place where you meet God - bleeding and dying on the Jericho road. It is only in that position that you can hear that word of liberation, **"Go, and do likewise."**

It was only after twelve disciples had abandoned their Lord and received His gracious forgiveness and reintroduction into fellowship that He could give them the great commission. Up until then it would have been an onerous burden to be borne by the flesh. After the final conversion it became their life.

This brings to mind

And Jesus answered him, "Simon, I have something to say to you." And he replied, "Say it, Teacher." "A moneylender had two

debtors: one owed five hundred denarii, and the other fifty. When they were unable to repay, he graciously forgave them both. So which of them will love him more?" Simon answered and said, "I suppose the one whom he forgave more." And He said to him, "You have judged correctly." (Luke 7:40-43)

This little parable is in the larger account of Luke 7:35-50: the sinner woman loved much because she had been forgiven much. She had met the Father at the point of His divine love, and was now able to move according to the measure she had received.

This truth ties us in with all the other scriptures on love

We love, because He first loved us. (1Jn 4:19)

For while we were still helpless, at the right time Christ died for the ungodly. For one will hardly die for a righteous man; though perhaps for the good man someone would dare even to die. But God demonstrates His own love toward us, in that while we were yet sinners, Christ died for us. (Rom 5:6-8)

If for a moment we would put God in the place of the lawyer we could ask, "Who did God have to love?"

Where would we be if He had asked that question?

Now think about the Christians who ask, "Who do I have to love?" "Who is my neighbor?" What would the church be if they recognized their neighbor as the One who showed mercy and went and did likewise? Not the do-gooderism of the liberal church, but the genuine compassion of those who have fully received the touch from the heart of the Father.

This parable also brings to mind the account of the woman taken in adultery (Jn 8:1f). The statement, **"Go, and sin no more"** comes just when Divine mercy has been applied. It comes not as a burden but as Divine empowerment. She leaves the presence of Jesus freed from who she was and is able to become who she never was, but was always meant to be. This principle helps us to see why the Christians of today are living with such depression and dullness: they have been forgiven, but have no idea of what they have been liberated from. They think they were liberated from the bad stuff they had done and that's all there is, and so instead of "**Go and sin no more**" being the divine liberation to live in newness of life, they go around thanking God for their salvation, yet living with the same low - grade sin condition that they always have had, which is absolutely terminal: deadly for the Church and deadly for the believer. Then their preachers think they are doing God a favor by telling these poor people that God does not care about sin and does not want them to talk about it. So there is no release, there is no liberation as a daily experience. They are told about all that God has done for them, that they are in fellowship with God and that the only thing to do is to wait for the next train out.

Paul said

For the law of the Spirit of life in Christ Jesus has set you free from the law of sin and of death. (Rm 8:2)

All that many people today know is judicial acquittal-charges dropped- and they still run around with the man of sin alive, alivin' and abreathin'. They never experience newness of life.

It is said, and scripturally so, that the problem with the Law is that we can't keep it. Paul said

Now we know that whatever the Law says, it speaks to those who are under the Law, so that every mouth may be closed and all the world may become accountable to God; because by the works of the Law no flesh will be justified in His sight; for through the Law comes the knowledge of sin. (Rom 3:19&20)

We get our definition of sin from the Law, and no one keeps the Law, because if we break it in one point we are guilty of all. So we have an impossible situation: we are all damned.

Now the popular gospel tells us that since the Law is so hard, God swooped down and gave us grace which is easy. Now I can dance along with nothing to disturb me, knowing that it is well with my soul. Period. Then out of the blue comes the word, **"Blessed are the poor in spirit."**

Now what am I going to do with that? If the Law was a rough schoolmaster, then this is impossible. "Do not kill" is swallowed up by, "Do not hate." "An eye for an eye" is swallowed up by **"love your enemies, do good to those who hate you" (Luke 6:27 b&c)**

Woe is me, for what the Law couldn't do to damn me the Sermon on the Mount completes. Right???

Let's look again at what Jesus says

"But love your enemies, and do good, and lend, expecting nothing in return; and your reward will be great, and you will be sons of the Most High; for He Himself is kind to ungrateful and evil men. Be merciful, just as your Father is merciful." (Lk 6:34&35)

"He Himself. . ." And as with the Parable of the Good Samaritan, (or maybe we should call it the Parable of the Guy on the Ground), our mercy- however little we may have of it- comes from Him. We give that which we have received from Him. His mercy is the source of our mercy. We love because He first loved us. We receive the revelation of the Father's love and the commandment to love, not as obligation, but it all comes out of, and back into, the Father. The point is not that we are going to love others and create a wonderful loving society. The point is that we will love as He has loved us and we will get our teeth kicked in, just as Jesus did. This will lead us deeper into the knowledge of the Lord: the fellowship of His sufferings. The fact that it doesn't work out according to our scenario is irrelevant; it didn't "work" for the Early Church-they got fed to the lions. But it did work to create a people who could prevail against the gates of hell. That, not some temporary triumph, is what matters.

We have talked thus far about the words of Jesus and how they come from the Father and are a revelation of the Father. We will now look at how the Holy Spirit works with the words of Jesus, because we have said that these words are more than "gotta do" words. We will see how God uses these words and makes them sources of power.

4

The Holy Spirit and the Words of Jesus

W HEN THE DAY OF PENTECOST had come, they were all together in one place. And suddenly there came from heaven a noise like a violent rushing wind, and it filled the whole house where they were sitting. And there appeared to them tongues as of fire distributing themselves, and they rested on each one of them. And they were all filled with the Holy Spirit and began to speak with other tongues, as the Spirit was giving them utterance. (Acts 2:1-4)

The scriptural record is short and concise: Jesus had completed His course on earth, had won reconciliation for mankind, ascended to the Father, and God now had residence in man. Man was now reconciled to God, and therefore God could dwell within the believer. **"They were all filled with the Holy Spirit."** The Holy Spirit was not some kind of religious influence; the Holy Spirit was God almighty, the third person of the Trinity, dwelling within.

With the coming of God in man, one would have expected changes - something would surely have been different. Much note has been taken of the supernatural powers that the apostles and some of the people moved in - tongues, healings, wisdom, and so forth - but it is almost with embarrassment that they note that the early Church started to keep the teachings of Jesus as well.

They were continually devoting themselves to the apostles' teaching and to fellowship, to the breaking of bread and to prayer. Everyone kept feeling a sense of awe; and many wonders and signs were taking place through the apostles. And all those who had believed were together and had all things in common; and they began selling their property and possessions and were sharing them with all, as anyone might have need. Day by day continuing with one mind in the temple, and breaking bread from house to house, they were taking their meals together with gladness and sincerity of heart, praising God and having favor with all the people. And the Lord was adding to their number day by day those who were being saved. (Acts 2:42-47)

Jesus had said, "Forsake all and follow me."

Jesus had said, "**Do not store up for yourselves treasures on earth,**"

Jesus had said, "seek first His kingdom and His righteousness,."

Not only were these being fulfilled, but these people were turning the other cheek, going the extra mile, preaching the good news, casting out demons, blessing those who cursed them, etc. Jesus' teachings were coming to life.

This was the immediate effect of the coming of the Holy Spirit, and it appears to be a spontaneous event without the influence of 2000 years of Church traditions; this is what happened when God met man. A new mode of life had been birthed- Church life, the life of the Spirit of God. Men forsook all and followed Jesus. Note that they did not go their own ways, sitting on pillars and forming monasteries, founding denominations and having seminars on the Holy Spirit; they lived according to the teachings that Jesus had left with them. The Sermon on the Mount was being empowered by the Holy Spirit who indwelt the believers. The Spirit and the Word were becoming one in the believer: spiritual fusion- the unlimited energy source.

But what was really going on?

Jesus had told them (two months earlier) that His teachings were intimately connected with the Holy Spirit.

"If you love Me, you will keep My commandments. I will ask the Father, and He will give you another Helper, that He may be with you forever; that is the Spirit of truth, whom the world cannot receive, because it does not see Him or know Him, but you know Him because He abides with you and will be in you." (John 14:15-17)

T HE HOLY SPIRIT was Jesus' promise to His disciples: He would leave but He would not leave them bereft: the Holy Spirit would come in His name. In fact it was vital that the Lord Jesus should leave.

"But I tell you the truth, it is to your advantage that I go away; for if I do not go away, the Helper will not come to you; but if I go, I will send Him to you. (John 16:7)

We did not need Jesus here as much as we needed the Holy Spirit here. This is the cold, hard fact. Jesus would have been outside us, teaching and governing. The Holy Spirit would be within us, teaching, leading, empowering, and above all, transforming. Jesus needed to be with the Father: He needed to ascend to the Father to receive the gift of the Holy Spirit.

"You heard that I said to you, 'I go away, and I will come to you.' If you loved Me, you would have rejoiced because I go to the Father, for the Father is greater than I." (John 14:28)

Jesus is clear that His union with the Father is vital to our long term well- being. This union of Jesus with the Father was necessary for the coming of the Holy Spirit.

"This Jesus God raised up again, to which we are all witnesses. Therefore having been exalted to the right hand of God, and having received from the Father the promise of the Holy Spirit, He has poured forth this which you both see and hear." (Acts 2:32&33)

Jesus received the promise of the Holy Spirit because the Father was joined with the Holy Spirit and He, Jesus, needed to go to the Father so the Spirit could be poured out in us. The Holy Spirit flows out of the union of the Father and the Son, and when they come into union then the Holy Spirit flows. We see this also in the book of Revelation

Then he showed me a river of the water of life, clear as crystal, coming from the throne of God and of the Lamb, in the middle of its street. On either side of the river was the tree of life, bearing twelve kinds of fruit, yielding its fruit every month; and the leaves of the tree were for the healing of the nations. (Rev 22:1)

That river is the Holy Spirit and He flows out of the union of the Father and the Son. How this affects us is seen in several places in John 14. Starting with the passage we saw a couple paragraphs ago.

"If you love Me, you will keep My commandments. I will ask the Father, and He will give you another Helper, that He may be with you forever; that is the Spirit of truth, whom the world cannot receive, because it does not see Him or know Him, but you know Him because He abides with you and will be in you." (Jn 14:15-17)

Notice the connection Jesus makes between the coming of the Holy Spirit and obedience to the commandments. "**If you love Me, you will keep My commandments**". Note the word, "**keep**." It does not say, "obey", it says, "**keep**," which entails not just the rote performance of them, but the guarding of them. Words are kept so that they dwell in the heart, and they remain there not as things I "gotta do," but as a treasured love letter from our beloved. When "**Love one another**" becomes a life giving word of the Father's love toward us, renewing our minds and transforming our lives, not only will we have more understanding of the Father, but Jesus will send the Comforter to us, teaching us and empowering us to make that word flesh. We will receive the Holy Spirit in a way that as of yet we have not. The word will come as the Father doing His works and the Son sending the Holy Spirit.

knowing, brethren beloved by God, His choice of you; for our gospel did not come to you in word only, but also in power and in the Holy Spirit and with full conviction; just as you know what kind of men we proved to be among you for your sake. (1Thess 1:4&5)

FATHER, SON AND Holy Spirit were at work in the proclamation of the Gospel. Truth was being spoken, and Paul shows them that it was not just the action of men, but the word itself was powerful. When the word that proclaims God is joined with faith, there is Divine activity there and then in the word itself.

For this reason we also constantly thank God that when you received the word of God which you heard from us, you accepted it not as the word of men, but for what it really is, the word of God, which also performs its work in you who believe. For you, brethren, became imitators of the churches of God in Christ Jesus that are in Judea, for you also endured the same sufferings at the hands of your own countrymen, even as they did from the Jews, (IThess 2:13&14)

When the word of God was preached by Paul, since it was the word of God, then these words of God

"Blessed are you when people insult you and persecute you, and falsely say all kinds of evil against you because of Me. Rejoice and be glad, for your reward in heaven is great; for in the same way they persecuted the prophets who were before you." (Mt 1:11&12)

are there as well. All truth is latent in the purely stated word of God. Paul was not telling them so much about being tough as he was telling them that God's power in Christ was sufficient for whatever might come. The power to endure was there in the word received by faith.

The gospel preached in so many pulpits today does not have the power and depth of truth to bring forth strength in God's people to stand through the difficulties. If we proclaim a word that does not perform a work, then the word we proclaim falls short of the truths of God. If our word is not a word in which God can dwell and act, then we do not work for the Kingdom of God. Paul was pointing out the work that the word did - both in the congregation and in the individual. As the well- known verse says,

For the word of God is living and active and sharper than any two-edged sword, and piercing as far as the division of soul and spirit, of both joints and marrow, and able to judge the thoughts and intentions of the heart. (Heb 4:12)

Going back to the passage in 1 Thessalonians, we want to note that the activity of God in the proclaimed word was used by Paul to prove to the Thessalonians that they were indeed elect of God. This is proof that God Almighty had a hand in their hearing of the word.

knowing, brethren beloved by God, His choice of you; for our gospel did not come to you in word only, but also in power and in the Holy Spirit and with full conviction; just as you know what kind of men we proved to be among you for your sake. (1Thess 1:4&5)

Note also that not only was God at work, but that Paul can use his own life as testimony to the validity of the word and work that was going on in that church. "You know what kind of men we proved to be among you." The witness to the word was divine, coming from the supernatural hand of God, but there was a human witness as well - not only were lives being transformed in the midst of the church there at Thessalonica, but a transformed man was at work in the delivery of that word. That was a supernatural work as well. Paul was not idly boasting. Many people will stand up in front of God's people saying, "Follow me," but few can truly add "as I follow Christ." Paul could make both statements. For now, we can only note that the success of the early Church had something to do with the kind of men who were preaching the gospel: the teachings of Jesus and the Holy Spirit had transformed them.

Such confidence we have through Christ toward God. Not that we are adequate in ourselves to consider anything as coming from ourselves, but our adequacy is from God, who also made us adequate as servants of a new covenant, not of the letter but of the Spirit; for the letter kills, but the Spirit gives life. (2Cor 3:4-6)

For Paul, the Spirit was inseparable from the word. He had lived with ritual for years. In his encounter with Christ, he met the full multi-dimensional Word of God. We'll return now to John's gospel and see another truth our Lord expresses about His words.

"He who has My commandments and keeps them is the one who loves Me; and he who loves Me will be loved by My Father, and I will love him and will disclose Myself to him." (John 14:21)

A few paragraphs back we saw in John 14:15 that the Holy Spirit would come to those who kept Jesus' commandments. Here, the keeping of His commandments is connected with Jesus revealing Himself. As we have His commandments and keep them, then He will disclose Himself to us. Now, what could be better than having Jesus disclose Himself to us? What is dearer to the heart of the believer than beholding the face of the Master? Jesus lays out clearly that if we keep His commandments, then the Father and the Son will love us. (We must remember - those words were the loving actions of the Father Himself). Jesus spoke and the Father was actively doing His work. Jesus spoke, and told us that

"If you abide in Me, and My words abide in you, ask whatever you wish, and it will be done for you. (John 15:7)

We are big on **"ask whatever you wish"** and short on **"If you abide in me and my words abide in you."**

Again, there is power in Jesus' words, both those that are in holy writ, and those that the Holy Spirit reminds us of as we go on in Christ. He makes little distinction between abiding in Him and His words abiding in us. We are not exonerated if we are saying we are in Him. We are powerless if both conditions are not met, because truly, it is not the one who jumps up and down about being saved who is the beloved one, it is the one in whom the truth is a living fountain of strength. In that person the love of God is completed.

And so it is glorious - as we turn the other cheek, go the extra mile, bless those who curse us, forsake the riches of this world. . . .

Yes, if we do these things we may find that we suffer reproach. Others may think we are stupid, naïve, or religious. They may not understand, or worse, may misunderstand. We may come to know Him not merely in the glory of obedience to His word, but in the fellowship of His sufferings. It may not be in the glory of success that we come to know Him, but in the agony of crying out to Him; in the distress of loss in the contradiction of sinners. . . In feeling a little of mankind's hatred of God directed at us, which is our privilege as His servants. And God is faithful to meet us there.

Judas (not Iscariot) *said to Him, "Lord, what then has happened that You are going to disclose Yourself to us and not to the world?" Jesus answered and said to him, "If anyone loves Me, he will keep My word; and My Father will love him, and We will come to him and make Our abode with him. He who does not love Me does not keep My words; and the word which you hear is not Mine, but the Father's who sent Me." (John 14:22-24)

So Judas (not Iscariot) asks Jesus what the difference is: how is Jesus going to reveal Himself to them and not to the others? What happens to make the difference?

Jesus replied simply that those who are His will do what He said. They will embrace His teachings, and the fruit of this will be that the Father and the Son will love them. Now, this is a particular kind of love. There were twelve whom Jesus loved, but then there was the disciple whom Jesus loved. **God so loved the world,** but He loved the Son. These loves differ in quality even as they differ in function, just as the love of a husband for his wife is different from the love of a gourmet for caviar. God can love in various degrees and various ways, and here it says that Father and Son love those who keep their commands. Notice that the commands Jesus gave are credited to the Father, not the Son - they are words of the Father, dear to His heart.

In the keeping of the commands by the believer, God has a resting place. If God said, "**Blessed are those who hunger and thirst for righteousness, for they shall be satisfied,**"(Mat 5:6) and we embrace that word in our hearts, and our faith joins with the word, then the Father has a point of fellowship with us in that word. Our love for righteousness becomes a place where we have fellowship with the Father. Just as music lovers have a place of fellowship with each other in their love of music - the more they love it the more they can talk and share - so it is with us and God: as we love those things that He loves, we have communion with Him. As the righteousness that is dear to His heart becomes dear to our hearts, we have fellowship - literally we share a common being. As we treasure the ways He moves, the qualities that please Him, then it is only natural that the Father should love us. He loves me as I keep His word, just as any father loves a son who keeps his word. This does not diminish His love for those for whom Christ died and are yet in darkness, but the scripture is clear that keeping Jesus' words is pleasing to God in a special way. This is not "works" in the negative sense, because my obedience is not being said to be propitiatory; that is the ongoing work of the blood of Christ. However, my faith in Him becomes deeper than a mere doctrinal assent or blind obedience led by fear. There is a special love for the Son that pleases the Father. Since He is pleased, He comes to dwell - and He does not come alone: the Son comes as well.

The commandments of Jesus are one of the main focal points of our communion with God. We cannot do what Christ did on Calvary; His blood had to open the way. Now that the door is open God commands us to believe, and that belief is embodied in our keeping the words that Jesus spoke; not just the doctrinal statements of His deity, but the words that Jesus received from the Father about the Kingdom of God.

The one who says, "I have come to know Him," and does not keep His commandments, is a liar, and the truth is not in him; but whoever keeps His word, in him the love of God has truly been perfected. By this we know that we are in Him: the one who says he abides in Him ought himself to walk in the same manner as He walked.

Beloved, I am not writing a new commandment to you, but an old commandment which you have had from the beginning; the old commandment is the word which you have heard. On the other hand, I am writing a new commandment to you, which is true in Him and in you, because the darkness is passing away and the true Light is already shining. (1Jn 2:4-7)

John tells us, probably years later, that the love of God has been perfected in the one who keeps the Lord's word. Notice where it says: "**In him.**" This indicates an internal work within the believer. God's love - both our love for God and the love of God toward us - has been perfected. To make sure that this is understood in its depth, he talks about the old commandment which was new to them a few years ago, being the word which was heard. The spoken and written commandment is an external word. This is what we can quantify and measure ourselves up against and say, "I am doing it." The new commandment that John is talking about is one "**which is true in Him and in you.**" No longer just God's word to us, an external thing that

God wants us to do, but an internal operation of God whereby the very inward purposes of God, the laws of His Spirit, have been written in our hearts.

"But this is the covenant which I will make with the house of Israel after those days," declares the LORD, "I will put My law within them and on their heart I will write it; and I will be their God, and they shall be My people. They will not teach again, each man his neighbor and each man his brother, saying, 'know the LORD,' for they will all know Me, from the least of them to the greatest of them," declares the LORD, "for I will forgive their iniquity, and their sin I will remember no more." (Jer 31:33&34)

This is a clear statement in the Old Testament, quoted twice in the book of *Hebrews*, and it is still God's purpose. We want what God can give us. God wants His Church to be a body of believers filled with His Spirit, yielded to His purposes. Jesus made it possible for that to come to pass by dying on the cross and now living to make intercession for us. His Spirit is within us leading us into all truth.

"These things I have spoken to you while abiding with you. But the Helper, the Holy Spirit, whom the Father will send in My name, He will teach you all things, and bring to your remembrance all that I said to you". (John 14:25&26)

What is the Holy Spirit going to remind us of? All that Jesus said. That is another reason we know that these teachings and commandments that Jesus gave are for the Church, now: the Holy Spirit is going to bring them back to us. The Holy Spirit is not going to let Jesus' teachings go to waste. He is not going to park them for 2000 years waiting for the next dispensation. If we are being led by the Holy Spirit, those words will be fulfilled, not because the Holy Spirit is whispering scriptures in our ears, not because He is quoting to us from the Bible, but because the Spirit knows the heart of God, even the deep things of God, and those things can be ministered by the Spirit to the inner man of those who have been regenerated.

John was writing a new commandment, "**which is true in Him and in you,**"

Jesus had prayed

"**O righteous Father, although the world has not known You, yet I have known You; and these have known that You sent Me; and I have made Your name known to them, and will make it known, so that the love with which You loved Me may be in them, and I in them.**" (John 17:25&26)

John's statement in 1 John 2 was an indication of the fulfillment of Jesus' prayer in John 17. Most Christians don't know, and most preachers don't care. God has opened His heart to us and given His Spirit to bear witness to the truth, to remind us of the truth, and to lead us into the truth. That is what He gave us to do, that is what He commanded us to be about:

"**Go therefore and make disciples of all the nations, baptizing them in the name of the Father and the Son and the Holy Spirit, teaching them to observe all that I commanded you; and lo, I am with you always, even to the end of the age.**" (Mt 28:19&20)

He wanted them to teach the nations "**to observe all that I commanded you.**"

5

THE TESTIMONY OF THE FATHER AND THE SON

S O WHAT DID JESUS SAY about what He had to say?

"For whoever is ashamed of Me and My words in this adulterous and sinful generation, the Son of Man will also be ashamed of him when He comes in the glory of His Father with the holy angels." (Mk 8:38)

"For whoever is ashamed of Me and My words, the Son of Man will be ashamed of him when He comes in His glory, and the glory of the Father and of the holy angels." (Lk 9:26)

There we have it twice. We receive Him, we receive His words. Jesus lumps them together- it's a package deal. We have no right to receive Him and not receive His words. If we claim to love Him yet repudiate His very heart - which is the heart of the Father - then we don't care about Him, only His benefits. If we are ashamed of Him or of turning the other cheek, forsaking all, going the extra mile, not rendering evil for evil, etc., then, on the day that matters most, He will be ashamed of us. Period. I am not allowed to pick and choose: He becomes my Lord, His ways - and they originate with the Father - become my way. Otherwise, He says, "Who is this guy?" when I walk up on Judgment Day.

"Not everyone who says to Me, 'Lord, Lord,' will enter the kingdom of heaven, but he who does the will of My Father who is in heaven will enter. Many will say to Me on that day, 'Lord, Lord, did we not prophesy in Your name, and in Your name cast out demons, and in Your name perform many miracles?' And then I will declare to them, 'I never knew you; DEPART FROM ME, YOU WHO PRACTICE LAWLESSNESS.' Therefore everyone who hears these words of Mine and acts on them, may be compared to a wise man who built his house on the rock. And the rain fell, and the floods came, and the winds blew and slammed against that house; and yet it did not fall, for it had been founded on the rock. Everyone who hears these words of Mine and does not act on them, will be like a foolish man who built his house on the sand. The rain fell, and the floods came, and the winds blew and slammed against that house; and it fell — and great was its fall." (Mt 7:21-27)

In verse 24 it says, "everyone who hears these words of Mine and acts on them". In verse 26 it says, "Everyone who hears these words of Mine and does not act on them." The kingdom of God is predicated on the Sermon on the Mount, and our Lord is emphatic on that. We have two passages that state that the record of our response to the teachings of the Lord will be strongly consulted on Judgment Day. In Mt 25, in the famous passage about the sheep and the goats, it says:

"But when the Son of Man comes in His glory, and all the angels with Him, then He will sit on His glorious throne. All the nations will be gathered before Him; and He will separate them from one another, as the shepherd separates the sheep from the goats; and He will put the sheep on His right, and the goats on the left. Then the King will say to those on His right, 'Come, you who are blessed of My Father, inherit the kingdom prepared for you from the foundation of the world. 'For I was hungry, and you gave Me something to eat; I was thirsty, and you gave Me something to drink; I was a stranger, and you invited Me in; naked, and you clothed Me; I was sick, and you visited Me; I was in prison, and you came to Me.' Then the righteous will answer Him, 'Lord, when did we see You hungry, and feed You, or thirsty, and give You something to drink? And when did we see You a stranger, and invite You in, or naked, and clothe You? When did we see You sick, or in prison, and come to You?' "The King will answer and say to them, 'Truly I say to you, to the extent that you did it to one of these brothers of Mine, even the least of them, you did it to Me.' (Mt 25:31-40)

Here, he does not refer to the Sermon on the Mount or to His teachings, but only to the essential content of His teachings. We will save for later the question about the Pauline Gospel and justification by faith, but make no mistake about it: the Pauline Gospel is rooted in the words of Jesus. The important thing for now is that the Son of God, Jesus Christ, into whose hands all judgment has been committed, says that it is important to keep His words: not just the doctrinal ones that keep us safe, but the practical ones that reveal His heart and show how we are to live.

"Heaven and earth will pass away, but My words will not pass away." (Mk 13:31)

The teachings that He received from the Father are not subject to dispensations, quibble, alteration, or the practical whining about how inconvenient they are; they are eternal words that were given to operate in a Body of regenerate people and to be empowered by the Holy Spirit- not human will power.

"Heaven and earth will pass away, but My words will not pass away." (Lk 21:33)

There it is a second time - and it did not change. They are not to be viewed as valid in the afterlife but merely discretionary now.

"Heaven and earth will pass away, but My words will not pass away". (Mt 24:35)

Oops - there we have it in triplicate; still no variation. And if we argue that as born again believers we are in a new realm, the fact is that even if heaven and earth have passed away and all things have become new, these are the words that abide.

"For He whom God has sent speaks the words of God; for He gives the Spirit without measure". (Jn 3:34)

So Jesus answered them and said, "My teaching is not Mine, but His who sent Me". (Jn 7:16)

"I have many things to speak and to judge concerning you, but He who sent Me is true; and the things which I heard from Him, these I speak to the world." (Jn 8:26)

These passages give us three times that Jesus attributes His words to the Father. We have already quoted several others in other chapters. They are not just referring to doctrinal statements about Himself, but also to the teachings that he gave - the Sermon on the Mount, the commands of discipleship, etc. These are the teachings or sayings. The word is the overall message that the sayings will lead us into, with the help of the Holy Spirit who comes in the name of the Son.

"I have come as Light into the world, so that everyone who believes in Me will not remain in darkness. If anyone hears My sayings and does not keep them, I do not judge him; for I did not come to judge the world, but to save the world. He who rejects Me and does not receive My sayings, has one who judges him; the word I spoke is what will judge him at the last day. For I did not speak on My own initiative, but the Father Himself who sent Me has given Me a commandment as to what to say and what to speak. I know that His commandment is eternal life; therefore the things I speak, I speak just as the Father has told Me." (Jn 12:46-50)

Over and over He attributes His words to the Father. The Father gave Him those words to give to us. These are the words of life.

At the end of His course, when all was finished and He was ready to ascend to the Father, Jesus said,

When they saw Him, they worshiped Him; but some were doubtful. And Jesus came up and spoke to them, saying, "All authority has been given to Me in heaven and on earth. Go therefore and make disciples of all the nations, baptizing them in the name of the Father and the Son and the Holy Spirit, teaching them to observe all that I commanded you; and lo, I am with you always, even to the end of the age." (Mt 28:17-20)

We have made multitudes of converts, but have we really made disciples? Can mere converts make disciples? How many people are willing to submit themselves to the process of discipleship that Jesus laid out? He did not ask them to go out and tell everybody about Himself: He told them to make disciples, and history shows that they did. We were commanded to show the nations living statements of Christ. If in fact the Church was functioning as a living statement of Christ, then more often the story would be as it was with the Philippian jailer who said, "What must I do to be saved?"

We were commanded to bring those words to the people in flesh and blood, and then lead those who received Him into the living fulfillment of those words. "Discipleship" is an overused, underdone word. The Lord Jesus is our standard and His words are the revelation of Himself. As these words are fulfilled in His Church, He has a platform for operation. Later on we will look very briefly at Church history and see how these words were influential in the life of the Church.

When Jesus laid out the way the Spirit would lead on earth, he placed great emphasis on His teachings. The witness of our Lord to the importance of His teaching should be sufficient, but since He attributed His words to the Father, it would stand to reason that the Father would have borne witness to the teachings of the Son. God spoke out very few times, but of the few times the He did speak out, He was clear about the importance of the teachings of Jesus. On the Mount of Transfiguration, after Peter was through blathering, the Father spoke,

While he was still speaking, a bright cloud overshadowed them, and behold, a voice out of the cloud said, "This is My beloved Son, with whom I am well-pleased; listen to Him!" (Mt 17:5)

Then a voice came out of the cloud, saying, "This is My Son, My Chosen One; listen to Him!" (Lk 9:35)

Then a cloud formed, overshadowing them, and a voice came out of the cloud, "This is My beloved Son, listen to Him!" (Mk 9:7)

The thrice repeated command – **"Listen to Him!"** Recognition was given to Him, **"This is My beloved Son"** and to His words, **"Listen to Him."** The Father affirmed Jesus and His words, in the same sentence.

So who is listening?

This revelation of the importance of the words of the Messiah broke no new ground - God had given Moses this understanding over a thousand years earlier.

"The LORD your God will raise up for you a prophet like me from among you, from your countrymen, you shall listen to him. This is according to all that you asked of the LORD your God in Horeb on the day of the assembly, saying, 'Let me not hear again the voice of the LORD my God, let me not see this great fire anymore, or I will die.' The LORD said to me, 'They have spoken well. I will raise up a prophet from among their countrymen like you, and I will put My words in his mouth, and he shall speak to them all that I command him. It shall come about that whoever will not listen to My words which he shall speak in My name, I Myself will require it of him.'" (De 18:15-19)

In this passage, well known to the Jews, Moses is quoting God. We know that they took great interest in this passage, because when the Jews came to John the Baptist

This is the testimony of John, when the Jews sent to him priests and Levites from Jerusalem to ask him, "Who are you?" And he confessed and did not deny, but confessed, "I am not the Christ." They asked him, "What then? Are you Elijah?" And he *said, "I am not." "Are you the Prophet?" And he answered, "No." (Jn 1:19-21)

Are you the prophet? They of course, were looking for another Elijah, but the scripture plainly told them to look for a teacher, of whom God said in the passage quoted above, "he shall speak to them all that I command him."

God gave Isaiah the same information that He gave Moses.

Although the Lord has given you bread of privation and water of oppression, He, your Teacher will no longer hide Himself, but your eyes will behold your Teacher. Your ears will hear a word behind you, "This is the way, walk in it," whenever you turn to the right or to the left. (Isa 30:20&21)

By Jesus' time, some of them did know that a teacher was coming. The woman at the well knew it,

The woman said to Him, "I know that Messiah is coming (He who is called Christ); when that One comes, He will declare all things to us." Jesus said to her, "I who speak to you am He." (Jn 4:25&26)

Jesus gave the people according to the needs and desires of their hearts. The Pharisees never got much of anything out of Him because their hearts were not right, while the multitudes got to see His miracles and wonder if He was a prophet or the Prophet or a deceiver or the Messiah. It is interesting to note, in the light of this, that Jesus never revealed His identity to anyone as directly as He did to a Samaritan woman who was looking for the Messiah who would declare all things.

These scriptures are witnesses to the fact that the Father testified concerning the teachings of our Lord. The Father gave the words to the Son and then told us to listen.

In the previous chapters I have attempted to fit the words of Jesus into the fellowship of the Father, Son, and Holy Spirit. We have laid out that these words are active, transforming revelations of the heart of the father that, when embraced in the heart of the believer and mixed with faith would draw the believer into fellowship with the Father, Son and Holy Spirit. There is always a spiritual context for these words, or else they become mere ethical teachings, like they did with Ghandi. Even on that level there is a lot of power in them, as Ghandi proved.

The teachings of Jesus were not given in isolation; they were the culmination of thousands of years of God's dealings with His people. In this chapter I have, perhaps, done a little violence to the record by taking them out of the living context they were given in, but I felt I would be remiss if I did not concentrate them and make us face the point blank reality of how strongly the Father and the Son regard these words, and how They relate them to Judgment Day.

However, there is more to the story. There would be more truth revealed, and the important things is to see how these teachings of Jesus fit into the fabric of the faith and life of the people of God, from the earliest dealing of God with His people, on through Church history, so that these teachings can once more assume their place in the life of the Church. We will begin with the Old Testament witness. If God gave Jesus these words, then these words should be in line with the other teachings that He had already given. We will look at the Old Testament for witnesses from the Father to the teachings of Jesus, and also to see how the Spirit of God was fitting these teachings into the life of His people.

6

WHAT JESUS SAW
WHEN HE READ THE
OLD TESTAMENT

"**W**OE TO YOU, SCRIBES AND **Pharisees, hypocrites! For you tithe mint and dill and cummin, and have neglected the weightier provisions of the law: justice and mercy and faithfulness; but these are the things you should have done without neglecting the others.**" (**Mt 23:23**)

One wonders what Bible Jesus was using; certainly the Pharisees did. They did not see things quite like Jesus saw them: after all, the whole thing was a gauntlet of pretty stiff requirements: tithes, sacrifices, dietary regulations, sanitation laws, health regulations, etc. It was not easy to be a Jew.

The Pharisees' views were the fruit of generations of traditions and interpretations, thousands of hours of study, consultation and prayer handed down, refined and debated among the rabbis and resulting in a comprehensive legal system. After that, Jesus comes along saying that the themes of the Law were justice and mercy and faithfulness. What did He know? After all, what could a Galilean carpenter know in the face of such long term consensus?

The stunning thing is that when we listen to modern preachers, with their neglect of the Old Testament and their off-hand way of reducing the Law to a list of mere regulations with no bearing on the modern Church, their view of the Old Testament is surprisingly similar to that of the Pharisees: they view it as a conglomeration of history, tradition, and do's and don'ts. They quote a few prophecies because they point to Christ, pull a few verses out of Daniel and the other prophets as being of future interest, and then set most of the Old Testament aside as an irrelevant bump on our road to salvation.

In contrast, for the New Testament writers, the Old Testament was a major source of inspiration. Paul derived his doctrine of justification by faith from a verse in Haggai and from the account of Abraham and Isaac in the Book of Genesis. Any Bible that gives Old Testament references in different typeface will show that the New Testament is full of quotes from the Old. This was not done just for polemical purposes- i.e. to prove a point- but it was because the Old Testament was the fountainhead of revealed truth. It was the Bible the Early Church used and from it they derived support for all the New Testament doctrines. The Early Church, patristic, medieval, and reformation attitudes toward the Old Testament were strictly according to what is plainly written in the New Testament.

For whatever was written in earlier times was written for our instruction, so that through perseverance and the encouragement of the Scriptures we might have hope. (Rom 15:4)

Now to Him who is able to establish you according to my gospel and the preaching of Jesus Christ, according to the revelation of the mystery which has been kept secret for long ages past, but now is manifested, and by the Scriptures of the prophets, according to the commandment of the eternal God, has been made known to all the nations, leading to obedience of faith; (Rom 16:25&26)

The Scripture, foreseeing that God would justify the Gentiles by faith, preached the gospel beforehand to Abraham, saying, "ALL THE NATIONS WILL BE BLESSED IN YOU." (Gal 3:8)

and that from childhood you have known the sacred writings which are able to give you the wisdom that leads to salvation through faith which is in Christ Jesus. All Scripture is inspired by God and profitable for teaching, for reproof, for correction, for training in righteousness; (2Tim 3:15& 16)

Not a single one of these scriptures is referring to the New Testament; it did not exist. The Old Testament is spoken of as having been "written for our instruction"; making known the gospel to the nations; as having "preached the gospel"; as being "profitable for teaching, for reproof, for correction, for training in righteousness"; and as being "able to give you the wisdom that leads to salvation through faith which is in Christ Jesus." Furthermore, all these quotes are from Paul who is often cited as an authority in minimizing the place of the Old Testament.

If we believed the literal interpretation of the New Testament, then when it talks about the Old Testament the case is clear. It is only when we let more contemporary religious ideas creep in that the Old Testament is relegated to the position of a relic. These words are vital to any discussion of the Gospel of Jesus Christ, just as Paul said.

When one hears talk about the Sermon on the Mount, one hears about idealism or impracticality; when one hears talk about the Old Testament Law, one hears talk of harshness. When Jesus talks about the Law, He sees **"justice and mercy and faithfulness."** In trying to see beyond the supposed harshness of the Law it is important to try to give some context to the words and to get it through twenty-first century brains that things were not what a casual glance might indicate. Let's take the example of slavery.

Slavery in the Old Testament is supposed to be an indication of the moral inferiority of the Law. We are told that these laws are from a more primitive age, before the great advances of the modern world had come about. Now while it is true that there are some Laws on slavery in Exodus that appear to merely ameliorate some of the abuses of the ancient system of slavery, many of the laws present a very different view.

"At the end of every seven years you shall grant a remission of debts. This is the manner of remission: every creditor shall release what he has loaned to his neighbor; he shall not exact it of his neighbor and his brother, because the LORD'S remission has been proclaimed. From a foreigner you may exact it, but your hand shall release whatever of yours is with your brother. However, there will be no poor among you, since the LORD will surely bless you in the land which the LORD your God is giving you as an inheritance to possess, if only you listen obediently to the voice of the LORD your God, to observe carefully all this commandment which I am commanding you today. For the LORD your God will bless you as He has promised you, and

you will lend to many nations, but you will not borrow; and you will rule over many nations, but they will not rule over you. If there is a poor man with you, one of your brothers, in any of your towns in your land which the LORD your God is giving you, you shall not harden your heart, nor close your hand from your poor brother; but you shall freely open your hand to him, and shall generously lend him sufficient for his need in whatever he lacks. Beware that there is no base thought in your heart, saying, 'The seventh year, the year of remission, is near,' and your eye is hostile toward your poor brother, and you give him nothing; then he may cry to the LORD against you, and it will be a sin in you. You shall generously give to him, and your heart shall not be grieved when you give to him, because for this thing the LORD your God will bless you in all your work and in all your undertakings. For the poor will never cease to be in the land; therefore I command you, saying, 'You shall freely open your hand to your brother, to your needy and poor in your land.'" (Dt 15:1-11)

The key to the whole thing is found in comparing verses 4 and 11. They apparently contradict, since the one says there will not be poor among you, while the other says that there will. However, in saying that there won't be poor among you, verse 5 adds, "if only you listen obediently to the voice of the LORD your God, to observe carefully all this commandment which I am commanding you today." If the level of giving among the Israelites is high enough, the abundance that the Lord provides will be sufficient for all, verse 6, "For the LORD your God will bless you as He has promised you." As the Law is fulfilled, then the blessing of the LORD will increase - whether it increases to every single family or not is irrelevant - and there will be no poor among the Israelites because those who are being prospered by the hand of the LORD will give to those who have little. The command to give will keep poverty away, and the people's obedience will bring down more abundance from God. The abundance will be sufficient for people to absorb the debts of others. As everyone gives freely, those who run into difficulties can count on help. There is no usury and therefore no compounding of debt. Society is kept in balance by principles of giving: the people give, and God gives.

From this commandment to give with an open hand, it is only an incremental step to the saying of Jesus

"Give, and it will be given to you. They will pour into your lap a good measure — pressed down, shaken together, and running over. For by your standard of measure it will be measured to you in return." (Lk 6:38)

We could also add Acts 2:45 and Acts 4:32-35.

Really it is not even an incremental step - the sayings of Jesus are fully inherent in these commands of Deuteronomy. The nation at large would receive according to their level of giving, God would bless a giving people; and Israel, the People of God, was to be that kind of people. Deuteronomy is concerned with the nation. Jesus is making sure that everyone understands that these principles apply to individuals as well. In any case, God's mode of blessing is seen to be constant in both the Old Testament and in Jesus' teachings.

'Now in case a countryman of yours becomes poor and his means with regard to you falter, then you are to sustain him, like a stranger or a sojourner, that he may live with you. Do not take usurious interest from him, but revere your God, that your countryman may live with you. You shall not give him your silver at interest, nor your food for gain. I am the LORD your God, who brought you out of the land of Egypt to give you the land of Canaan and to be your God'. (Lev 25:35-38)

An open heart was to be a hallmark of the Children of Israel. Money lending was not to be a business, but rather giving was to be a virtue, a way of life. Jesus would say later,

"But love your enemies, and do good, and lend, expecting nothing in return; and your reward will be great, and you will be sons of the Most High; for He Himself is kind to ungrateful and evil men." (Lu 6:35)

Again, that is a commentary on the verse in Leviticus. He is retelling the law according to the heart that gave it. We are not called to philosophize about the poor - they were no different in those days than they are now. They were neither more diligent nor less, neither more ambitious nor less, neither more worthy of compassion nor less; they were the poor.

Going back to that passage in Deuteronomy 15 we see that debts were not allowed to pile up; after seven years, out they go. God did not want people who were nonfunctional buried under a mountain of debt; it leads to exploitation by the rich, and it transfers the burdens of one generation to the next. (Witness the national debt of every country in the Western World). There was to be no ongoing cycle of poverty.

Not only did God not want the nonfunctional buried under debt, He did not want the exploiters to have an ongoing method of perpetual growth. These principles are often seen as primitive, but they are the only laws that take full account of human nature and give a people a chance to maintain a long-term prosperity.

But maybe we've gotten ahead of ourselves: the principle about debt is wonderful, but what about slavery? Where do we find justice, mercy and faithfulness in that?

"If your kinsman, a Hebrew man or woman, is sold to you, then he shall serve you six years, but in the seventh year you shall

set him free. When you set him free, you shall not send him away empty-handed. You shall furnish him liberally from your flock and from your threshing floor and from your wine vat; you shall give to him as the LORD your God has blessed you. You shall remember that you were a slave in the land of Egypt, and the LORD your God redeemed you; therefore I command you this today. It shall come about if he says to you, 'I will not go out from you,' because he loves you and your household, since he fares well with you; then you shall take an awl and pierce it through his ear into the door, and he shall be your servant forever. Also you shall do likewise to your maidservant. It shall not seem hard to you when you set him free, for he has given you six years with double the service of a hired man; so the LORD your God will bless you in whatever you do. (Dt 15:12-18)

In the ancient world, if you got into debt you could be sold into slavery. Sounds brutal, and as practiced in most cultures it was terrible. The thought of any kind of slavery resounds in our minds as contrary to all humanitarian principles; an evil worse than the debtors' prisons in England. That was an institution that survived 1800 years of Christianity. In the enlightened 21st century we give our poor a little welfare and let them live and raise their children in a slum. That's after 2000 years of Christianity.

Maybe we should look a little deeper into the Old Testament system.

Okay, for example I'm in debt over my head. That's a pretty neat trick since debts are forgiven every seven years. But maybe that part of the Law isn't being fulfilled and debts are being allowed to accumulate long periods of time. Or perhaps I did manage to pull it off in just three years; maybe I'm a wastrel and I bet the farm in Las Vegas and lost. Well, since the land was given to my family by lot at the command of the LORD, and technically the land belongs to the LORD, at least I cannot lose the family patrimony. My children will eventually get the land back.

'The land, moreover, shall not be sold permanently, for the land is Mine; for you are but aliens and sojourners with Me. Thus for every piece of your property, you are to provide for the redemption of the land.

If a fellow countryman of yours becomes so poor he has to sell part of his property, then his nearest kinsman is to come and buy back what his relative has sold'. (Lev 25:23-25)

Poverty is not automatically bequeathed on my descendants. The land, however, may have to be let out till the jubilee year. If I have a relative to help, they can pay my debts, give me my land back on their terms, and help me get my life in order; this was the work of the kinsman redeemer. The family was legally given first option to help. They would most likely be most knowledgeable of my personal problems and most able to apply correction where it was needed. Breaking the cycle of poverty was to begin in the family if possible, and these laws helped to give the legal authority to step in and help.

Lacking a relative, the land could be sold (i.e. rented until the jubilee) to someone. If there was still a debt, I, with my family, could go into slavery to that person.

Ahh. . . here's the brutal part. . .

But wait - what did the Law in Deuteronomy 15 say?

It says he will serve you for six years and go free in the seventh year, and that he would be well supplied out of the abundance the Lord would provide. He could begin again and have more than sufficient for a new start. He was to be blessed in his going. Hopefully those years had been a positive time. God certainly wanted them to be.

'If a countryman of yours becomes so poor with regard to you that he sells himself to you, you shall not subject him to a slave's service. He shall be with you as a hired man, as if he were a sojourner; he shall serve with you until the year of jubilee. He shall then go out from you, he and his sons with him, and shall go back to his family, that he may return to the property of his forefathers. For they are My servants whom I brought out from the land of Egypt; they are not to be sold in a slave sale. You shall not rule over him with severity, but are to revere your God'. (Lev 25:39-43)

He was to be shown respect. Perhaps he sort of became like one of the family. In any case, his previous incompetence or stupidity or plain misfortune did not lead him into a life of crime, but into the household of a prosperous family where for six years he learned to get out of bed at a good hour (six days a week), he learned to work, he learned to take care of tools, he learned accountability. The master who bought him was under divine instruction to be careful with him. The system was supposed to be so merciful that provision was made for him to stay on if he and the master were in agreement. One would only have wanted to stay on if things were good.

If seen with an understanding of justice, mercy and faithfulness, the whole thing makes our criminal justice system look brutal. Ample provision was made for the redemption of those with difficulties; the family was given that first chance. Only then was opportunity given to someone with the means to take the person in, train him to work, and then send him out to try again. If he liked his master, the master could sign him on. This was how it was supposed to be.

This is all well and good, but what about the most brutal law of all - where the kid is hauled before the elders of the town, taken out and stoned? Let's take a look at that through the eyes of justice, mercy and faithfulness.

"If any man has a stubborn and rebellious son who will not obey his father or his mother, and when they chastise him, he will not even listen to them, then his father and mother shall seize him, and bring him out to the elders of his city at the gateway of his hometown. They shall say to the elders of his city, 'This son of ours is stubborn and rebellious, he will not obey us, he is a glutton and a drunkard.' Then all the men of his city shall stone him to death; so you shall remove the evil from your midst, and all Israel will hear of it and fear". (Deut 21:18-21)

Let's first of all remember how the Lord intended this: it is not happening before strangers in the halls of justice in New York City; it is taking place in the village or town (or neighborhood if it is a large city) where the family has lived for generations, and the neighbor families have lived with this family for decades. Everybody knows what's up. Only the father and the rebellious son don't have eyes to see it in perspective, so when they show up at the gate with the father dragging the son, we might hear one of the following:

"Well, you know you've been awful hard on him these last few years - ever since you fell on hard times. I think you ought to lighten up on him."

Or maybe,

"Well, he did get drunk a couple times and cussed you out but you know, I'd be surprised if a few sober people hadn't cussed you out, and you've been overly tipsy a few times yourself."

Or possibly the oldest and wisest of them spoke up,

"You really haven't been much of a father to him. I need a couple workers for a project, and I think I could help him."

Of course, it was possible that the consensus was, "Well, ever since he was fifteen we've had to keep our houses locked, our tools hidden, and our daughters out of sight. We've seen your struggles with him, and we think you've tried everything, and so have we."

If that was the consensus, then there was no joy in that town that night; one of their hopes for the future had been executed. It was not just a blot on the family, but they as the people of God had all failed, and all hearts had to be bared before God. A son who had grown up in their midst, who had gone to feasts with them, had sat under the Levite teachers, had shared the joys of harvest, and had also shared the hardships of lean times, was now under the ground. As they had thrown the stones they had to search their own hearts: "Did I give the family support?" "Was I a good influence?"

Sure, some of them might have been glad to be rid of a trouble–maker, but it was also true that there would have been a few uncles, and perhaps a few cousins among the stone throwers. It most certainly would not have been done casually. Yes, he might have been eliminated before he actually killed or raped someone and earned the death sentence. In ancient times disregard for family, neighbors, and divinely given laws was not allowed to play itself out in society. Some might call it harsh, but it is infinitely more merciful than anything in place today, and there was much less likelihood for a miscarriage of justice here. These things would not have been done in haste, and they were done with the knowledge that God was watching. They were done on the principle that a heart full of hate was the heart of a murderer; a heart full of lust is the heart of an adulterer; a heart full of covetousness is the heart of an idolater. New Testament principles are plainly behind even this.

Notice also that the Law dictated impartial justice for all: even the stranger and the alien were to have justice, or else.

'When a stranger resides with you in your land, you shall not do him wrong. The stranger who resides with you shall be to you as the native among you, and you shall love him as yourself, for you were aliens in the land of Egypt; I am the LORD your God'. (Lev 19:33&34)

No narrowness here: those who dwelt among the Children of Israel as strangers were to be loved. Earlier in the chapter stands the famous verse

You shall not take vengeance, nor bear any grudge against the sons of your people, but you shall love your neighbor as yourself; I am the LORD. (Lev 19:18)

When the Pharisee asked Jesus who his neighbor was, he was simply playing games, because he knew that later on the chapter tells us who, besides their neighbor, people are "to love as themselves": the stranger. We have already seen who He was. This agrees with the teachings of our Lord; all the teachings in the Bible are to point us to Christ.

'And when did we see You a stranger, and invite You in, or naked, and clothe You? When did we see You sick, or in prison, and come to You?' "The King will answer and say to them, 'Truly I say to you, to the extent that you did it to one of these brothers of Mine, even the least of them, you did it to Me.'" (Mt 25:38-40)

These were some of the principles of justice, mercy and faithfulness that God intended to establish in Israel when He gave the Law. Build a society on these principles and it would revolutionize the world. Isaiah, who understood the intent of the Law, saw nations coming to Israel and pouring out their treasures because of the wisdom and beauty of a people who kept the heart of the Law.

"For behold, darkness will cover the earth
And deep darkness the peoples;
But the LORD will rise upon you
And His glory will appear upon you.
Nations will come to your light,
And kings to the brightness of your rising.

Lift up your eyes round about and see;
They all gather together, they come to you.
Your sons will come from afar,
And your daughters will be carried in the arms.
Then you will see and be radiant,
And your heart will thrill and rejoice;
Because the abundance of the sea will be turned to you,
The wealth of the nations will come to you." (Isaiah 60:2-5)

The world would see righteousness, mercy, and faithfulness, and it would be astonished. There would be a God-taught people who would lead the nations into the life and ways of God. This is basic Old Testament teaching. The New Testament would take this understanding and open it up to the world by taking it out of the hands of an individual nation and placing it in the hands of those who had faith: the Church. The outline did not change: there would still be a people, a flesh and blood expression of the living God on this earth.

By the time of Jesus the country was run by the Romans, and the Jews did not have control over their country. The nation that could offer sacrifices, maintain the temple, and supervise the keeping of the pilgrim feasts was coming to an end. The line of kings who could have implemented these laws on the national level did not have access to the throne. But what was important was the heart behind the Law: the heart of the Father. The Father's heart had never been clearly revealed to the world by the nation of Israel because the Law was spiritual, and the people were totally of flesh. Jesus came, then, to supersede the Law, to reveal its heart, and empower those who were of faith to possess the kingdom that the Father had prepared. They would do this by the power of the Holy Spirit Whom God sent to lead them. This is pure Old Testament doctrine straight from the pens of Matthew, Paul and John.

Obedience to the Old Testament laws had been the condition for the people of Israel to stay in the promised land: in like manner, the Sermon on the Mount laid out the conditions for the eternal people of God, the Church, to inherit the full blessing of God. Justice, mercy, and faithfulness are here seen to be the cornerstones of that kingdom, even in its Old Testament expression, just as Jesus said.

One other thing we need to note - the Divine Signature of the Lord. He does not say, "Love your neighbor as yourself." What He says is

you shall love your neighbor as yourself; I am the LORD. (Lev 19:18b)

When God gives a commandment and adds, "**I am the LORD,**" there has to be a reason. In the first place, we have cited repeatedly the teaching of Jesus that, "**Out of the abundance of the heart the mouth speaks,**" so that we know that the commandment is from the heart of God. Secondly, the LORD pronounced the divine name in giving this commandment. That name was not spoken casually: Moses sat in a crag of a rock to hear a complete statement of the Name in one of the high points of his life. The Name was so holy that the Jews forgot how to pronounce it. The Name was representative of the person in ways that the western mind will never grasp. The name spoke of the nature of the person, so when at the end of a commandment the Lord says, "**I Am the Lord**", this has extreme significance. If we want the window into the heart of God, any commandment that ends, "I am the LORD," is that window.

'**Now when you reap the harvest of your land, you shall not reap to the very corners of your field, nor shall you gather the gleanings of your harvest. Nor shall you glean your vineyard, nor shall you gather the fallen fruit of your vineyard; you shall leave them for the needy and for the stranger. I am the LORD your God**'. (Lev 19:9&10)

That is a window on the divine economy: the poor are to have a chance at the remaining fruit and grain because GOD SAID SO. It's as if He said, "The poor are to have a provision because I, not Baal, am God." The corners of the fields were to be left unharvested because the Law of Yahweh is law, not the Constitution nor the Bill of Rights nor the Civil Code. This commandment is an expression of God's heart, not some idea that Moses came up with to solve the problem of poor in the land. "**I am the LORD**," is here spoken with the full authority and resolve of the Almighty God. Again,

'**You shall not hate your fellow countryman in your heart; you may surely reprove your neighbor, but shall not incur sin because of him. You shall not take vengeance, nor bear any grudge against the sons of your people, but you shall love your neighbor as yourself; I am the LORD**'. (Lev 19:17&18)

The heart is to be clear of hatred toward anyone. We are not to take vengeance. These commandments come from the Heart of God. We are not the ones to take actions - especially if we are angry - other than to reprove the wrongdoer. Our hearts are not to harbor the sins committed against us in the past. We judge other people by the standard with which we judge ourselves. Freedom from rancor has its source in God: He is not up there itching for the day when He can get back at everyone who has maligned His name; if He were we'd all be in the Lake of Fire by now. He is awaiting the day when He can avenge the wrongs done to His servants, not out of human anger or bitterness, but in a way that is commensurate with His righteousness. Since the divine justice has waited for the day when things will be made right, so can we. The day of wrath awaits the full realization of the mercy of God, and that takes time.

"But love your enemies, and do good, and lend, expecting nothing in return; and your reward will be great, and you will be sons of the Most High; for He Himself is kind to ungrateful and evil men." (Lk 6:35)

He has been kind to the ungrateful and evil men, and we have hated Him for it. He has been longsuffering and we have despised Him for it. His failure to take revenge has been a major source of unbelief throughout the ages. Humankind has been quick to judge when He has been slow. The Old Testament abounds in examples of God's boundless love. Let's look at another of them.

"You shall not oppress a stranger, since you yourselves know the feelings of a stranger, for you also were strangers in the land of Egypt." (Ex 23:9)

One wonders how God knows so much about this business of strangers. It was deliberate on His part that His people should have had that experience early in their formation; that the culture, the traditions and writings should be imbued with the remembrance of those early difficult days of a nation being born in the midst of an alien culture and then experiencing deliverance. They were expected to remember those feelings.

"But if a stranger sojourns with you, and celebrates the Passover to the LORD, let all his males be circumcised, and then let him come near to celebrate it; and he shall be like a native of the land. But no uncircumcised person may eat of it." (Ex 12:48)

In order to be an Israelite, not just a naturalized citizen, one had merely to keep the Law, just like natural born Israelites had to. Circumcision was the entrance for the males (rather stiff requirement to be sure, but the same for all) but once there, the person was treated like the native born, whether of Jewish parentage or not. No exclusivity, no worrying about genealogy, heritage, etc. A person became native born, or shall we say was consecrated native born. We could almost say he was "born again" into the Jewish nation. That person was a child of Abraham whether his parents were or not. Membership in Israel was never on the basis of race: it was always on the basis of covenant: keep the covenant and you're in, don't keep the covenant and you are out- even if your genealogy is perfect. God was not prejudiced: the door was open, and any who wanted to be a son could enter. The book of *Hebrews* would later tell us it was through faith.

These Old Testament teachings were an example of merciful Laws. Leaving the gleanings for the poor, careful treatment of your enemy's ox, not holding a person's cloak in pledge, ordinances to keep the rich from plundering the poor- all of these were merciful laws. The "Sermon on the Mount" kind of ethics is found in various places in the Old Testament. It was not pulled down out of the sky by Jesus. Anything that came from God would reflect these principles, whether black and white, or flesh and spirit. It so happens that they stand in black and white in the Old Testament, and red and white in the New Testament.

In *Job*, his righteousness was not that of scrupulously keeping the commandments or the offering of sacrifices - all of which he, in fact, did. But that was not his righteousness. We see as he gives his defense

"Because I delivered the poor who cried for help,
And the orphan who had no helper.
The blessing of the one ready to perish came upon me,
And I made the widow's heart sing for joy.
I put on righteousness, and it clothed me;
My justice was like a robe and a turban.
I was eyes to the blind And feet to the lame.
I was a father to the needy,
And I investigated the case which I did not know.
I broke the jaws of the wicked
And snatched the prey from his teeth." (Job 29:12-17)

Job's defense here was that he fulfilled the righteousness of the Old Testament Law and the prophets, not that he used sacrifice as a cover for his own ungodly ends. Caring for the widow and orphan, helping the blind, etc, all were basic elements of the Old Testament. In chapter 31 we have several examples:

"I have made a covenant with my eyes;
How then could I gaze at a virgin?"(Job 31:1)

Compare that with

"You have heard that it was said, 'YOU SHALL NOT COMMIT ADULTERY'; but I say to you that everyone who looks at a woman with lust for her has already committed adultery with her in her heart." (Mt 5:27&28)

Job had seen the danger and had stayed clear.

"If I have kept the poor from their desire,
Or have caused the eyes of the widow to fail,

Or have eaten my morsel alone, And the orphan has not shared it

(But from my youth he grew up with me as with a father,
And from infancy I guided her),
If I have seen anyone perish for lack of clothing,
Or that the needy had no covering,
If his loins have not thanked me,
And if he has not been warmed with the fleece of my sheep,
If I have lifted up my hand against the orphan,
Because I saw I had support in the gate,
Let my shoulder fall from the socket,
And my arm be broken off at the elbow." (Job 31:16-22)

Compare that with Jesus' commands

And He also went on to say to the one who had invited Him, "When you give a luncheon or a dinner, do not invite your friends or your brothers or your relatives or rich neighbors, otherwise they may also invite you in return and that will be your repayment. But when you give a reception, invite the poor, the crippled, the lame, the blind, and you will be blessed, since they do not have the means to repay you; for you will be repaid at the resurrection of the righteous." (Luke 14:12-14)

Or again with John the Baptist's command:

And he would answer and say to them, "The man who has two tunics is to share with him who has none; and he who has food is to do likewise." (Lk 3:11)

For that matter, it is in line with the prophetic text which speaks about the true fast unto the LORD.

"Is it not to divide your bread with the hungry
And bring the homeless poor into the house;
When you see the naked, to cover him;
And not to hide yourself from your own flesh?" (Isa 58:7)

All these are of the same essence. There is no differentiation between Old and New Testaments. Again, Job calling down a curse upon himself:

"If I have put my confidence in gold,

And called fine gold my trust,

If I have gloated because my wealth was great,

And because my hand had secured so much;" (Job 31:24&25)

Compare that with

"No one can serve two masters; for either he will hate the one and love the other, or he will be devoted to one and despise the other. You cannot serve God and wealth." (Mt 6:24)

We could add the parable of the rich fool to the New Testament comparison: greed was not part of Job.

"Have I rejoiced at the extinction of my enemy,

Or exulted when evil befell him?

No, I have not allowed my mouth to sin

By asking for his life in a curse." (Job 31:29&30)

Compare with

"You have heard that it was said, 'YOU SHALL LOVE YOUR NEIGHBOR and hate your enemy.' But I say to you, love your enemies and pray for those who persecute you, so that you may be sons of your Father who is in heaven; for He causes His sun to rise on the evil and the good, and sends rain on the righteous and the unrighteous. (Mt 5:43-45)

Job understood that the heart of the matter was the heart, just as it says elsewhere:

'Oh that they had such a heart in them, that they would fear Me and keep all My commandments always, that it may be well with them and with their sons forever!' (Deut 5:29)

"Hear, O Israel! The LORD is our God, the LORD is one! You shall love the LORD your God with all your heart and with all your soul and with all your might. These words, which I am commanding you today, shall be on your heart." (Deut 6:4-6)

Some would object that Job was justifying himself on the basis of having kept that Law, but Job was not "keeping the Law," He was living by faith, just like in the book of *Hebrews* where it writes about Moses,

By faith he kept the Passover and the sprinkling of the blood, so that he who destroyed the firstborn would not touch them. (Heb 11:28)

He offered the sacrifice that God commanded in the Law, but he was walking before God, and not just under obligations, and that is faith. Moses was one of the heroes of faith even as he kept the Law.

The Bible tells us to serve God out of our hearts, not out of ritual obligations, because the words themselves are words of life that are to be planted deep within the believer, and are to bring forth the full understanding of God's purposes

"He humbled you and let you be hungry, and fed you with manna which you did not know, nor did your fathers know, that He might make you understand that man does not live by bread alone, but man lives by everything that proceeds out of the mouth of the LORD." (Dt 8:3)

The book of *Hebrews* quotes from *Jeremiah* 31 several times:

"Behold, days are coming," declares the LORD, "when I will make a new covenant with the house of Israel and with the house of Judah, not like the covenant which I made with their fathers in the day I took them by the hand to bring them out of the land of Egypt, My covenant which they broke, although I was a husband to them," declares the LORD. "But this is the covenant which I will make with the house of Israel after those

days," declares the LORD, "I will put My law within them and on their heart I will write it; and I will be their God, and they shall be My people. They will not teach again, each man his neighbor and each man his brother, saying, 'Know the LORD,' for they will all know Me, from the least of them to the greatest of them," declares the LORD, "for I will forgive their iniquity, and their sin I will remember no more." (Jer 31:31-34)

His Law needs to be deep within the heart of the believer, not as commands for sacrifice and offering, but as a living power that brings each one to the experiential knowledge of God. This begins with the forgiveness of sins so that the Spirit and the word can have a pure dwelling place and bring about the renewing of the mind and heart. Ultimately this will produce a God–taught people. He places His words in the heart, and we live by them because His words are spirit and they are life. The words of the Lord's mouth have come to us from His heart, and they are not merely commandments to be mindlessly followed, but in them the veil is pushed back and the purposes of the Father are revealed more fully. Regenerate hearts can receive those words and bring about a holy people consecrated to the Lord through the grace of God. This is plain Old Testament teaching, though the power had not yet been given in Old Testament times. The New Testament brings everything into focus so that we may see the person and work of Christ in clarity.

Many more examples foreshadowing the teachings of Jesus could be drawn from the Old Testament: the prophets are full of them, more are in Proverbs, more are to be found in the Law, all of which indicate that the Old Testament bears full witness to the Sermon on the Mount, and that the essence truly is justice, mercy and faithfulness, just as our Lord said.

We ignore these parts of the Scripture to our own loss. In these days of moral decline, the truths our Lord's teachings reveal are a great strengthening in the struggle for true Spirit-inspired holiness. If we are not concerned with holiness, then we are not concerned with God, because no one will see God without holiness.

Follow peace with all men, and holiness, without which no man shall see the Lord: (Heb 12:14 AV)

But have nothing to do with worldly fables fit only for old women. On the other hand, discipline yourself for the purpose of godliness; for bodily discipline is only of little profit, but godliness is profitable for all things, since it holds promise for the present life and also for the life to come. (1 Tim 4:7&8)

Many churches have relegated much of the Sermon on the Mount, as well as most of the Old Testament to the reliquary because of a total misinterpretation of the writings of the apostle Paul, to which we now turn. The church has tended to put most of Paul's writings in that reliquary as well, but at least those parts of Paul's epistles are in like- minded company, as we shall see.

7

THE WORDS OF JESUS
AND THE APOSTLE PAUL

Paul is the great revolutionary: he took on the established powers of his day; his gospel endures to the present, freeing us from the religious world of works and law and allowing us to soar in the heavens in untrammeled freedom. Liberty is his hallmark, gunning down everything of organization, ritual, and tradition.

This is a caricature, and as with most caricatures, the problem is one of exaggeration. Unfortunately for this caricature, its very popularity betrays its chief flaw: it is too molded to fit the temper of the times; there is more twentieth century to it than there is Paul. The twentieth century was the great century of the individual (the twenty-first is proving to be more group oriented) valuing the iconoclast: the solitary individual fighting against group tyranny. The reality of Paul is one of a builder, a man who joined people together, establishing them with their feet on the ground, with solid doctrinal foundations, joined together in the work of the gospel, firmly rooted in the teachings of Jesus. Those teachings permeate his doctrine, his approach to ministry, and the life of the churches that he established. He built his churches on eternal truth, so they could endure the test of time in a very hostile environment, having the presence of God with them. That is why so many churches today which claim the Pauline gospel as their chief inspiration fall so short of the mark: Paul's scope was bigger than personal justification. It permeated the totality of life and did not bow to the culture of the day, therefore it was able to give the individual a firm place in society, in family, and in the Church.

Paul's ministry began with a dramatic encounter on the road to Damascus. Up to that time his only knowledge of the Way was that it was a group of Jews who taught against the Law of Moses as their founder had, and lived according to the teachings of that founder.

They were continually devoting themselves to the apostles' teaching and to fellowship, to the breaking of bread and to prayer. Everyone kept feeling a sense of awe; and many wonders and signs were taking place through the apostles. And all those who had believed were together and had all things in common; and they began selling their property and possessions and were sharing them with all, as anyone might have need. Day by day continuing with one mind in the temple, and breaking bread from house to house, they were taking their meals together with gladness and sincerity of heart, praising God and having favor with all the people. And the Lord was adding to their number day by day those who were being saved. (Acts 2:42-47)

Their way was simple. We tend to speak of the "primitive Church," contrasting it with the more complex church that evolved, as if there was a lot more that God had in mind than that first outworking of the Holy Spirit; as if our volumes of theology and a church on every corner and our great mass media ministries are a major advance over the second chapter of Acts; as if our great halls full of complacent people who know they are saved and will meet Jesus someday way out there are a great advance over these simple Jewish believers who had already met Jesus and had been shaken to the core by Him. Back then, multitudes came to Christ through the simple testimony of the apostles and the demonstration of His power and life. What Saul of Tarsus saw when he looked at the followers of Jesus was all simple and it was revolutionary. It was not what anyone - least of all Saul - had expected.

Like all the Jewish intelligentsia, Saul had it all figured out: God was not the originator of this stuff; good people who followed the Law of Moses did not operate like this.

And the congregation of those who believed were of one heart and soul; and not one of them claimed that anything belonging to him was his own, but all things were common property to them. And with great power the apostles were giving testimony to the resurrection of the Lord Jesus, and abundant grace was upon them all. For there was not a needy person among them, for all who were owners of land or houses would sell them and bring the proceeds of the sales and lay them at the apostles' feet, and they would be distributed to each as any had need. Now Joseph, a Levite of Cyprian birth, who was also called Barnabas by the apostles (which translated means Son of Encouragement), and who owned a tract of land, sold it and brought the money and laid it at the apostles' feet. (Acts 4:32-35)

It was kind of like that passage in Leviticus, with all this giving and sharing, and there was breaking bread from house to house as well. This was the fulfillment of what Jesus had said from the beginning.

Jesus said to him, "If you wish to be complete, go and sell your possessions and give to the poor, and you will have treasure in heaven; and come, follow Me." (Mat 19:21)

"Do not store up for yourselves treasures on earth, where moth and rust destroy, and where thieves break in and steal. But store up for yourselves treasures in heaven, where neither moth nor rust destroys, and where thieves do not break in or steal;" (Mat 6:19)

"So then, none of you can be My disciple who does not give up all his own possessions". (Luke 14:33)

The Holy Spirit was bringing about the life of Jesus in the midst of these "primitive believers," the Sermon on the Mount was being fulfilled, God's kingdom was now, and they were part of it. The miraculous was there, as Jesus had said it would be, and the gospel was preached. These events were so amazing that Jerusalem was all abuzz. Saul of Tarsus would certainly have heard of these occurrences: they were not done in a corner. Processing this way of life and these teachings would have been even more difficult for him than for the messengers that John the Baptist had sent to Jesus a couple years before.

At that very time He cured many people of diseases and afflictions and evil spirits; and He gave sight to many who were blind. And He answered and said to them, "Go and report to John what you have seen and heard: the BLIND RECEIVE SIGHT, the lame walk, the lepers are cleansed, and the deaf hear, the dead are raised up, the POOR HAVE THE GOSPEL PREACHED TO THEM. Blessed is he who does not take offense at Me." (Luke 7:21–23)

94

Saul of Tarsus saw a lot of the same things that John's messengers saw; he understood none of them. There were reports of amazing miracles, just as there had been with the Galilean. There was a lot of talk about love, and they certainly did seem to reach out to the needy. These people were not anti-temple, in fact, they appropriated one corner of it for themselves, although the Galilean had reportedly talked of doing away with the Temple. They still offered sacrifices, (for that had not been fully clarified, and it would be Paul, many years later, who would do that; they had not worked out the theological implications of the death, burial, and resurrection of Christ). Their manner did not seem to be quite like anything in Saul's experience, or like anything in the history of the Jewish nation. He could not see anything in these occurrences but a dismaying repudiation of the traditions that were sacred to the Jews.

Interestingly enough, these things are also an inscrutable mystery for most modern Christians. Perhaps they show the first blush of God's love for us: a unique outpouring (certainly!), with strange manifestations that just came and went, totally unprepared for and unique to that time (certainly not!). Whatever our reaction to the first four chapters of Acts, there is one unshakable thing that all can see in the midst of the early Church: the operation of the Holy Spirit. As we noted in our chapter on the Holy Spirit and the words of Jesus: the Spirit was moving and producing in those early believers the fulfillment of the teachings of Jesus.

After his conversion, Paul disappeared for a few years - if we may call fourteen years "a few years." Meanwhile the Church grew and multiplied as a branch of Jewish faith. When Barnabas finally made the break in Antioch and established a

Gentile Church, he called in Saul. "The rest," as they say, "is history."

After Paul became a believer he reshaped Christian theology. He showed how the door between Jew and Gentile was battered down, and we were all recognized as one Body in Christ. But where in Paul's preaching were the words of Jesus? Jesus did not talk about justification by faith. Reconciliation was there in Jesus' teachings, "**first be reconciled to your brother**," but not like in Paul's "**through Him to reconcile all things to Himself.**" Paul's book of *Colossians* is cosmic in scope; Jesus' teachings were within a simple framework that could be understood by the ignorant and unlearned as well as (or better than) by the educated. Jesus did not talk about God imputing faith as righteousness. Jesus did not talk about breaking down the barrier between Jew and Gentile in Christ. To so many, there is a great chasm between the teachings of Jesus and the teaching of Paul.

Paul, however, did talk about love. His teachings about the Body of Christ were far closer to Planet Earth than the Mystical Body concept attributed to him. Paul would rhapsodize about being transformed by the renewing of the mind, but a few verses down the page we see:

Let love be without hypocrisy. Abhor what is evil; cling to what is good. Be devoted to one another in brotherly love; give preference to one another in honor; not lagging behind in diligence, fervent in spirit, serving the Lord; rejoicing in hope, persevering in tribulation, devoted to prayer, contributing to the needs of the saints, practicing hospitality.

Bless those who persecute you; bless and do not curse. Rejoice with those who rejoice, and weep with those who weep. Be of the same mind toward one another; do not be haughty in

mind, but associate with the lowly. Do not be wise in your own estimation. Never pay back evil for evil to anyone. Respect what is right in the sight of all men. If possible, so far as it depends on you, be at peace with all men. Never take your own revenge, beloved, but leave room for the wrath of God, for it is written, "VENGEANCE IS MINE, I WILL REPAY," says the Lord. BUT IF YOUR ENEMY IS HUNGRY, FEED HIM, AND IF HE IS THIRSTY, GIVE HIM A DRINK; FOR IN SO DOING YOU WILL HEAP BURNING COALS ON HIS HEAD. Do not be overcome by evil, but overcome evil with good. (Rom 12:9-21)

This is what the Sermon on the Mount looks like after the Holy Spirit has run it through the heart of an apostle and it comes through that grinder as bread to feed Christ's sheep. No, it's not what Jesus said on a word for word basis, but it is the very essence of it: turning the other cheek, going the extra mile, forgiving one's enemies, feeding the poor, etc. This is the fulfillment of the words of the Law, the words of the prophets, and the words of Jesus.

We theological Western beings think that this is the periphery, the extra stuff thrown in to smooth over problems in the Church and keep behavior under control; the kind of thing thrown out by the stars of the show to give the groundlings something to think about. To Paul, this was the reason for justification: that these bodies might be presented to God as living sacrifices. Justification was never meant to be about heaven; that is a modern sales pitch to fill church pews and allay weak consciences. In Paul's own thinking, all the words about justification, all his teachings about grace, all the things he said about being free from the Law, were to bring us together: Jews and Gentiles, slave and free, man and woman, so that the law of love might be carried out by a Spirit-led people.

The redeeming work of Christ was to bring us all into the Kingdom, and once there, Jesus tells us what that kingdom looks like. It is the same kingdom for Jews and Gentiles. It is the same kingdom in this dispensation and that dispensation. As with the speed of light, it is constant for all viewers at all times. "By faith Abel. . .", "by faith Moses. . .", by faith you. . ., by faith I. . .; it's all the same. It's one Lord, one faith, one baptism, or we repudiate the Book of Ephesians.

Justification, reconciliation, salvation, all these things are elements of the gate through which access is given into the Kingdom of God. Once there, the words of Jesus describe the territory, and as those words are lived, they are the foundation upon which the house is built, and as we have seen in John 14-16, they are the summons to the Father to come and indwell the house.

Jesus answered and said to him, "If anyone loves Me, he will keep My word; and My Father will love him, and We will come to him and make Our abode with him." (John 14:23)

There are many other verses that say the same thing.

Paul's emphasis to those who are now part of the Lord's Body is not that they live with an expectation of being carried away, but he emphasizes a practical life:

Instruct those who are rich in this present world not to be conceited or to fix their hope on the uncertainty of riches, but on God, who richly supplies us with all things to enjoy. Instruct them to do good, to be rich in good works, to be generous and ready to share, storing up for themselves the treasure of a good foundation for the future, so that they may take hold of that which is life indeed. (1 Tim 6:17-19)

This is perfectly in line with the Sermon on the Mount – and Deuteronomy 15. Many modern believers wouldn't attribute that theology to Paul at all; they would say that it contradicts Paul's teachings because it has something to do with works. The fact of the matter is that this type of saying permeates the writings of Paul.

For by grace you have been saved through faith; and that not of yourselves, it is the gift of God; not as a result of works, so that no one may boast. For we are His workmanship, created in Christ Jesus for good works, which God prepared beforehand so that we would walk in them. (Eph 2:8-10)

We are not saved by works; we were saved for them. He that denies the "**for**" is not upholding the "**by**" either. Grace was for one purpose: that the works of Christ might be visible on this earth in His Church. His redeeming work is visible when you

"Let your light shine before men in such a way that they may see your good works, and glorify your Father who is in heaven". (Mt 5:16)

Paul was on the same page with the Lord on all of his teaching. The Lord did not tell Paul something different than he told the disciples when He walked the earth, He expanded it. Jesus had already said that

"Heaven and earth will pass away, but My words will not pass away". (Mt 24:35)

His words were the words of heaven, those words were the heart of the Father, and they were the words that Jesus received from the Father. Our modern tendency to lump them all together as "works" is entirely contrary to Paul. In fact, the etherealization of Paul's doctrine is the most serious stumbling block among believers today. We preach a caricature of justification by faith so that there is nothing to restrict our freedom of movement. We want to know our freedom in Christ, our position in Christ, our security in Christ; in fact, we want to know those things a lot more than we want to know Christ. We subscribe to theologies that leave the earth and other people out of the life of the believer. That's how we like it; nothing to do but save others and wait for the future to arrive. The Pauline Gospel, however, is that now that we have been justified, the life of the Spirit stands open before us; and if we walk by the Spirit we will not fulfill the lusts of the flesh, but the result will be what we saw in Romans 12:9 and following. Those teachings will be fulfilled beyond the letter.

Paul knew the place of works in the scheme of things, having smashed into the brick wall in his years as a Pharisee.

For this reason also, since the day we heard of it, we have not ceased to pray for you and to ask that you may be filled with the knowledge of His will in all spiritual wisdom and understanding, so that you will walk in a manner worthy of the Lord, to please Him in all respects, bearing fruit in every good work and increasing in the knowledge of God; (Col 1:9&10)

Now may our Lord Jesus Christ Himself and God our Father, who has loved us and given us eternal comfort and good hope by grace, comfort and strengthen your hearts in every good work and word. (2Th 2:16&17)

All Scripture is inspired by God and profitable for teaching, for reproof, for correction, for training in righteousness; so that the man of God may be adequate, equipped for every good work. (2Tim 3:16&17)

Saul the Pharisee had tried to enter God's house through good works, or more specifically works of the Law. Paul the believer was now in that house through God's endeavor, and now as a resident of that house, Paul now had the power to please God, and he also had the understanding of what would please

Him. For the first time in his life, good works were a possibility. Up until then all had been the knowledge of good and evil. Up till then the old man was running him, and the Law only gave fuel to the religious part of the fallen nature: the more he had tried to serve God, the tighter the noose of sin became. The Law that was to lead him to life had become a fountain of death. After his encounter with Jesus, the grace in which he was able to live became a fountain of power enabling him to live by the faith of the Son of God. Paul now had the power to serve God in a spiritual way, and Paul was intent on leading his converts into that life of service, that life of fellowship, that life of worship of God that Jesus had proclaimed in His earthly ministry and now had made available through His blood. The words of Jesus were part of the bedrock of the Christian life.

The book of 1Corinthians provides some example of the teachings of Jesus that Paul applied by the Spirit to some problems in the Church. Concerning lawsuits

Actually, then, it is already a defeat for you, that you have lawsuits with one another. Why not rather be wronged? Why not rather be defrauded? (1Cor 6:7)

Jesus had told His disciples to bear the loss, now Paul does. When there was a question about divorce

But to the married I give instructions, not I, but the Lord, that the wife should not leave her husband (but if she does leave, she must remain unmarried, or else be reconciled to her husband), and that the husband should not divorce his wife.

But to the rest I say, not the Lord, that if any brother has a wife who is an unbeliever, and she consents to live with him, he must not divorce her. (1Cor 7:10–12)

Where the Lord had spoken- and you can read it in Matthew 5:32- then things were settled. Where the Lord had said

101

nothing, then apostolic wisdom, given by the Spirit, was in order.

When there was a question about the Lord's Supper, then

For I received from the Lord that which I also delivered to you, that the Lord Jesus in the night in which He was betrayed took bread; and when He had given thanks, He broke it and said, "This is My body, which is for you; do this in remembrance of Me." In the same way He took the cup also after supper, saying, "This cup is the new covenant in My blood; do this, as often as you drink it, in remembrance of Me." (1Cor 11:23-25)

If the Lord sovereignly gave that to Paul, then it was the same thing He gave Luke. In any case, Jesus' words settled the question, as they should. And furthermore it is interesting to note that the Gospels of Luke and Mark were written by men who were deeply involved in the Gentile mission. Mark was in it from the beginning with his uncle Barnabas, and Luke accompanied Paul on numerous journeys. He also wrote the history of the early Church. These men knew Paul's theology and got straight from him the importance of the teachings of our Lord for the new churches that were coming into being. This testifies strongly and clearly to Paul's view of the importance of Jesus' words to the life of the Church.

When there was a question about finances for the apostles,

So also the Lord directed those who proclaim the gospel to get their living from the gospel. (1Cor 9:14)

As it is written

"Stay in that house, eating and drinking what they give you; for the laborer is worthy of his wages. Do not keep moving from house to house". (Lk 10:7)

Paul knew very well how Jesus had taught his disciples to travel and minister. This was the standard. He goes out of his way to explain how he did not do that, in order to fulfill a higher principle - that of giving

What then is my reward? That, when I preach the gospel, I may offer the gospel without charge, so as not to make full use of my right in the gospel.

For though I am free from all men, I have made myself a slave to all, so that I may win more. (1Cor 9:18 &19)

Jesus told them to just go and spread the word, taking no thought. When the Spirit led Paul to stay in a place, he worked so that he might fulfill

"Give, and it will be given to you. They will pour into your lap a good measure — pressed down, shaken together, and running over. For by your standard of measure it will be measured to you in return." (Lk 6:38)

In 2 Corinthians the issue was Paul's ministry. Was he an apostle? What was the proof of his apostleship? Much of his defense was based on the words of Jesus. Jesus' disciples would suffer persecution.

"Blessed are those who have been persecuted for the sake of righteousness, for theirs is the kingdom of heaven. Blessed are you when people insult you and persecute you, and falsely say all kinds of evil against you because of Me. Rejoice and be glad, for your reward in heaven is great; for in the same way they persecuted the prophets who were before you." (Mt 5:10–12)

Paul had suffered much - in fact more than the others; therefore he regarded himself as being among the blessed.

but in everything commending ourselves as servants of God, in much endurance, in afflictions, in hardships, in distresses, in beatings, in imprisonments, in tumults, in labors, in sleeplessness, in hunger, in purity, in knowledge, in patience, in kindness, in the Holy Spirit, in genuine love, in the word of truth, in the power of God; by the weapons of righteousness for the right hand and the left, by glory and dishonor, by evil report and good report; regarded as deceivers and yet true; as unknown yet well-known, as dying yet behold, we live; as punished yet not put to death, as sorrowful yet always rejoicing, as poor yet making many rich, as having nothing yet possessing all things. (2Cor 6:4-10)

This is the very picture of a follower of Jesus according to Jesus' words. Paul was not ashamed to say, "in everything commending ourselves as servants of God, . . ." because his gospel of grace made fidelity to Jesus the way of life, and not ritual obedience to dead letter. Obviously it was his faith that justified him. Nevertheless he could say that these works showed him as a servant of Jesus Christ. The life he lived showed who his Lord was. Faith was not an abstract acceptance of a theological fact; it was the ongoing life of service to the living Lord. Paul's faith had footsteps, just as father Abraham's did. He did not consider these dead works and for us to do so is to misconstrue Paul's gospel, to misconstrue faith, and to misconstrue the very nature of Christian life. These words were within the framework that Jesus laid out for His disciples: travelling from city to city, taking nothing with them, regarding high and low equally, proclaiming the gospel freely, etc.

Even in his theology, the words of Jesus are the bedrock. In his depiction of Christ's death in Philippians, the principles that Christ preached were the principles that Paul used to describe the sacrifice of Jesus.

Let this mind be in you, which was also in Christ Jesus: Who, being in the form of God, thought it not robbery to be equal with God: But made himself of no reputation, and took upon him the form of a servant, and was made in the likeness of men: And being found in fashion as a man, he humbled himself, and became obedient unto death, even the death of the cross. Wherefore God also hath highly exalted him, and given him a name which is above every name: That at the name of Jesus every knee should bow, of things in heaven, and things in earth, and things under the earth; And that every tongue should confess that Jesus Christ is Lord, to the glory of God the Father. (Php 2:5-11AV)

Here Jesus took the lowest seat, humbled Himself that He might be exalted, lost His life that He might find it, left His Father, gave all that He had, bore others' burdens, loved God with all His heart, mind and soul, and loved His neighbor (you!) as Himself. Jesus' life is depicted as the fulfillment of His own words.

And when Paul says "Let this mind be in you, which was also in Christ Jesus:" how dare we insult intelligence to say that we are exhorted to have His mind, but that the words that came from that mind are for another dispensation!!!

After a lengthy examination of justification by faith, Paul in Galatians 5, returns to the Christian life,

For in Christ Jesus neither circumcision nor uncircumcision means anything, but faith working through love. (Gal 5:6)

Ultimately, preventing circumcision was never the issue. Jettisoning the Law was never the issue. Paul will see it fulfilled the only way it can be, and that is faith working through love, as he says a few verses down:

For you were called to freedom, brethren; only do not turn your freedom into an opportunity for the flesh, but through love serve one another. For the whole Law is fulfilled in one word, in the statement, "YOU SHALL LOVE YOUR NEIGHBOR AS YOURSELF." (Gal 5:13&14)

It is still of vital importance that the Law be fulfilled, but you don't have to know the Law to fulfill it, you just have to let the Spirit lead you beyond the Law into life.

Compare the essence of Paul's depiction of the fruit of the Spirit with the essence of Jesus' depiction of Kingdom of heaven values: the Beatitudes. Is there a difference in essence between

"Blessed are the poor in spirit, for theirs is the kingdom of heaven." (Mt 5:3) and saying **"The fruit of the Spirit is love"?**

Will the poor in spirit be anything else but love? Will love produce anything but a person poor in spirit, never accumulating for self, but always giving to God and neighbor?

"Blessed are those who mourn, for they shall be comforted." (Mt 5:4) to be compared with "the fruit of the Spirit is joy"?

Shall the comfort of the mourners be anything but Spirit-produced joy, and won't they that have the fruit of the Spirit have joy set before them so that they may endure?

"Blessed are the gentle, for they shall inherit the earth. (Mt 5:5) To be compared with "the fruit of the Spirit is peace?

Are not gentleness and peace companions in the righteous?

We could go down the whole list, comparing the work of the Spirit with the beatitudes and, though it would be forcing it to try to find a one-to-one correspondence, nevertheless, Paul saw the Holy Spirit's witness to Jesus' words very clearly. The Spirit will produce the same essence of life in the believer as Jesus depicted in the Sermon on the Mount. Just go down the two lists: nine beatitudes and nine fruits, one Lord, one Spirit. Whether it's Paul teaching on slaves or teaching about the mysteries of the faith, the teachings of Jesus are there, infusing Paul's words. So many today have taken a few chapters out of the beginning of Paul's epistles, added a few verses against sexual sin, thrown in the passages on prophecy and the last days, and created a gospel that does nothing to touch life today. We give devotional significance to the rest of Paul's writings: feel

106

good soothing words that were originally supposed to be sharp points used by the Spirit to knit the Church together. We create a synthesis that leaves 21st century affluent materialism unscathed, but diligently criticizes the kind of sin that the rest of the world delights in - and we wonder why the world does not come running to the people of God to hear divine wisdom.

It would not be hard to write a book similar to this one, talking about the words that God gave Paul, and how the modern church ignores them, picking and choosing verses at will and ignoring others that Paul, at least, thought were important. Interestingly enough, many of those words of Paul are largely his God-given restatement of Christ's teachings. Since the gospel is spirit and not letter, Paul is at liberty to seek the fresh restatement of those words as the times and circumstances dictate. Jesus had said:

Jesus answered and said to him, "If anyone loves Me, he will keep My word; and My Father will love him, and We will come to him and make Our abode with him. He who does not love Me does not keep My words; and the word which you hear is not Mine, but the Father's who sent Me.

"These things I have spoken to you while abiding with you. But the Helper, the Holy Spirit, whom the Father will send in My name, He will teach you all things, and bring to your remembrance all that I said to you. ' (Jn 14:23-26)

Notice that the Holy Spirit will bring to remembrance all that Jesus said; that is in the dispensation of the Spirit; that is one of His works. The Holy Spirit will bring to remembrance the very words that some say do not even pertain to the dispensation of the Spirit.

Yes, Paul was given more revelation from the Holy Spirit: Jesus said that there were things the disciples were not at that

107

time ready to bear, and that those things would be revealed. It was given to Paul to clarify and unveil many things: the relation of Jew and Gentile, the redemption, the Body of Christ, the heading up of all things in Christ, etc. Granted all of these things, our intellectual adherence to these doctrines does not absolve us or our churches from the sin of having ignored so much that is vital and original with Paul, as well as having wrongly used Paul's gospel as justification for ignoring the Sermon on the Mount and yielding all of Christian life to the dominating influences of this age.

But what about the heart of Paul's gospel?

The nagging question still persists - what about justification by faith? Paul is emphatic that it is faith that justifies, and that works have no part.

The best way to answer what is an intellectually dishonest question is to refer modern readers to Paul's own words, and point out to them the tension that is in those words if modern definitions of "faith" are allowed to prevail. The modern churches have bent Paul out of recognition, undermining much that was central to Paul, in their quest to make the Gospel palatable to the masses and cater to the individualizing tendencies of our culture. Consider

For no man can lay a foundation other than the one which is laid, which is Jesus Christ. Now if any man builds on the foundation with gold, silver, precious stones, wood, hay, straw, each man's work will become evident; for the day will show it because it is to be revealed with fire, and the fire itself will test the quality of each man's work. If any man's work which he has built on it remains, he will receive a reward. If any man's work is burned up, he will suffer loss; but he himself will be saved, yet so as through fire. (1Cor 3:11-15)

More than a few preachers could not preach on that passage if their souls depended on it. If they did, they would use rhetorical tricks to say that it does not mean what it says, or that it wasn't written to Christians.

Therefore do not go on passing judgment before the time, but wait until the Lord comes who will both bring to light the things hidden in the darkness and disclose the motives of men's hearts; and then each man's praise will come to him from God. (1Cor 4:5)

Everyone who competes in the games exercises self-control in all things. They then do it to receive a perishable wreath, but we an imperishable. (1Cor 9:25)

With good will render service, as to the Lord, and not to men, knowing that whatever good thing each one does, this he will receive back from the Lord, whether slave or free. (Eph 6:7& 8)

For we must all appear before the judgment seat of Christ, so that each one may be recompensed for his deeds in the body, according to what he has done, whether good or bad. (2Cor 5:10)

Whatever you do, do your work heartily, as for the Lord rather than for men, knowing that from the Lord you will receive the reward of the inheritance. It is the Lord Christ whom you serve. For he who does wrong will receive the consequences of the wrong which he has done, and that without partiality. (Col 3:23-25)

For it is written, "AS I LIVE, SAYS THE LORD, EVERY KNEE SHALL BOW TO ME, AND EVERY TONGUE SHALL GIVE PRAISE TO GOD." So then each one of us will give an account of himself to God. (Rom 14:12)

Do not be deceived, God is not mocked; for whatever a man sows, this he will also reap. For the one who sows to his own flesh will from the flesh reap corruption, but the one who sows to the

Spirit will from the Spirit reap eternal life. Let us not lose heart in doing good, for in due time we will reap if we do not grow weary. So then, while we have opportunity, let us do good to all people, and especially to those who are of the household of the faith. (Gal 6:7&8)

Paul in no way challenges the belief in a system of rewards; we the faithful will be rewarded for the good we do. Our good however, is not the basis for our salvation, for that is of God. Its source is God, and He gives it to those who rely on Him. Our works don't achieve it, they cannot merit it, because it is from God. However, our place in Christ never absolves us from the responsibility of service, it does not release us from cause and effect - what we sow we reap - but it places us in the domain of the Spirit, where God can be served in the way that pleases Him. For the first time God can be served in a spiritual way by a spiritual people. For the first time the love of God can be seen in bodily form in a multitude of people. For the first time God's people have power to live a life that reveals to heaven and earth the nature of the Father.

So that the manifold wisdom of God might now be made known through the church to the rulers and the authorities in the heavenly places. (Eph 3:10)

For the first time "Thy will be done on earth as it is in heaven" is possible. That is why Jesus died. That divine life now opened up to us is the Holy City to which he has transported us; only the godless would cheapen that reality with "Do we have to?"

Our new birth gives us the power to continue in the Spirit, but it does not guarantee that we will. Our new birth gives us access to the life of God, but that does not mean that we will use what we have been given. Paul's exhortation about sowing and reaping was not given to unbelievers; it was given to churches, and is both a promise of blessing and a warning of judgment. We are saved by grace, through faith, but an unfortunate number will be saved, as Paul says it, "**so as through fire.**"

If anyone advocates a different doctrine and does not agree with sound words, those of our Lord Jesus Christ, and with the doctrine conforming to godliness, he is conceited and understands nothing; (1Tim 6:3&4a)

8

Church History and the Words of Jesus

THE HISTORY OF THE CHURCH affords us many examples of the Lord blessing those who acknowledged Jesus and his words. The scope of this book does not permit us to give many details but at least a few examples are in order.

We have already noted how that when the Holy Spirit fell on the Jerusalem Church, the result was a completion of the words of Jesus: the Sermon on the Mount came to life. The exorbitant giving, the forsaking of material goods, the bonding together of many people for the Kingdom of God, and the perseverance in the face of persecution were all exactly what the Lord taught. The rest of Acts gives a few glimpses of the same characteristics.

Consider Dorcas, spending herself making clothes for others. Consider the Church in the house where Peter showed up after his prison release episode - complete with a room full of people who didn't really believe Peter could be at the door. Consider the young (?) men travelling with Paul: Aristarchus, Luke, Epaphroditus, Titus, Timothy. They went out taking nothing for the journey. The churches they founded and upheld were founded on the teachings of Jesus. The churches of Macedonia were a good example. In 2 Corinthians we see that a poor people gave sacrificially for the saints in Jerusalem:

Now, brethren, we wish to make known to you the grace of God which has been given in the churches of Macedonia, that in a great ordeal of affliction their abundance of joy and their deep poverty overflowed in the wealth of their liberality. For I testify that according to their ability, and beyond their ability, they gave of their own accord, begging us with much urging for the favor of participation in the support of the saints, and this, not as we had expected, but they first gave themselves to the Lord and to us by the will of God. (2Cor 8:1-5)

This is a perfect fusion of the gospel of Paul with the teachings of our Lord. The giving, the joy, the spontaneous outpouring are all hallmarks of the teachings of Christ in the Synoptic Gospels. All are equally hallmarks of the effects of the Holy Spirit in the midst of the Church, as Jesus had said they would be. To call this "grace," to say, "**we wish to make known to you the grace of God which has been given in the churches of Macedonia,**" is so characteristic of Paul's concept of grace and so alien to our own. He talks about that offering the same way a lesser person would have talked about a healing or some other miracle. But here is Paul's astonishment - nay wonder - at the transforming power of God just because the Holy Spirit freed some people to give utterly beyond themselves, and to encounter the grace of God in the midst of the act. Awesome! Not just giving monetarily, but a heightened awareness of God and a deep appreciation of the gift that Paul's apostolic gift was to them. What modern preacher could talk about a collection like that - and it wasn't even to enlarge his own ministry.

Later on in 2 Corinthians we see:

And He has said to me, "My grace is sufficient for you, for power is perfected in weakness." Most gladly, therefore, I will rather boast about my weaknesses, so that the power of Christ may dwell in me. Therefore I am well content with weaknesses, with insults, with distresses, with persecutions, with difficulties, for Christ's sake; for when I am weak, then I am strong. (2Cor 12:9&10)

The same principle is at work in:

"Whoever exalts himself shall be humbled; and whoever humbles himself shall be exalted". (Mt 23:12)

"Whoever then humbles himself as this child, he is the greatest in the kingdom of heaven". (Mt 18:4)

All of this accords with the principle, "The first shall be last and the last first."

The Book of Philippians abounds in examples of putting others first: whether it is Paul eschewing death because his life was more necessary for the Church, or the picture of Christ humbling Himself, or Timothy, of whom Paul says:

But I hope in the Lord Jesus to send Timothy to you shortly, so that I also may be encouraged when I learn of your condition. For I have no one else of kindred spirit who will genuinely be concerned for your welfare. For they all seek after their own interests, not those of Christ Jesus. (Php 2:19-21)

Or again, Epaphroditus:

Receive him then in the Lord with all joy, and hold men like him in high regard; because he came close to death for the work

of Christ, risking his life to complete what was deficient in your service to me. (Php 2:29&30)

A greater contrast with the ministry of today would be hard to find. Many of today's ministry have more in common with the clergy of the Middle Ages than they do with Paul and his group of young men.

Now I praise you because you remember me in everything and hold firmly to the traditions, just as I delivered them to you. (1Cor 11:2)

And what traditions might those be? Who might the giver of the Gospel of Grace be receiving "traditions" from? I thought he was against all tradition.

Therefore when you meet together, it is not to eat the Lord's Supper, for in your eating each one takes his own supper first; and one is hungry and another is drunk. What! Do you not have houses in which to eat and drink? Or do you despise the church of God and shame those who have nothing? What shall I say to you? Shall I praise you? In this I will not praise you. (1Cor 11:20-22)

When Paul chews out the church at Corinth because of people getting drunk and others being gluttons at their dinners together, this has no application to today because the context for it no longer exists: our lives don't come together that much. We don't join like that as a regular part of Church life. Jesus had led them toward interlocked lives of love. The modern theology is individual and fragmented. Paul said to the Thessalonians:

For even when we were with you, we used to give you this order: if anyone is not willing to work, then he is not to eat, either. For we hear that some among you are leading an undisciplined life, doing no work at all, but acting like busybodies. Now such persons we command and exhort in the Lord Jesus Christ to work in quiet fashion and eat their own bread. (2Th 3:10-12)

116

Here they are either eating together or feeding the poor. Both of these are regular functions of Church life if you believe Jesus and Paul. Our modern gospel has little to say about any of this; the New Testament Church operated on different principles. The exhortation to eat their own bread was not an encouragement to our current state of affairs where everyman eats his own bread all alone - if he has any.

When we go beyond the book of Acts most modern Christians are at a loss. The earliest of the Church fathers - sometimes known as the Apostolic Fathers- are not read much anymore because their works are, well. . . boring. They just exhort people to. . . well. . . follow the Sermon on the Mount, page after page.

The *Didache*, sometimes known as the *Teaching of the Twelve*, was very highly regarded by the early Church. This document harks back to the earliest days of the Church when there were still itinerant prophets travelling the countryside and each local gathering had a plural eldership. From chapter one we learn that:

"There are two ways, one of life, the other of death, and there is a great difference between the two ways. The way of life is this. First of all thou shalt love the God that made thee: secondly, thy neighbor as thyself. And all things whatsoever thou wouldest not have befall thyself, neither do thou unto another. Now of these words the doctrine is this. Bless them that curse you, and pray for your enemies and fast for them that persecute you; for what thanks is it if ye love them that love you? Do not even the Gentiles do the same? But do ye love them that love you? Do not even the Gentiles do the same? But do ye love them that love you and ye shall not have an enemy. Abstain thou from fleshly and bodily lusts. If any man give thee a blow to the

*right cheek, turn to him the other also, and thou shalt be perfect;
if any man impress thee to go with him one mile, go with him
twain; if any man take away they cloak, give him thy coat also."
(Didache 1- Lightfoot)*

And so on it goes; an early summery of the Sermon of
the Mount. Chapter two gives us a rundown of the Ten Commandments and some other basic moral principles, and then
in the middle of chapter three we read:

*"Thou shalt not turn away from him that is in want, but
shall make thy brother partaker in all things, and shall not say
that anything is thine own. For if ye are fellow partakers in that
which is imperishable, how much rather in the things which are
perishable?" (Didache 3- Lightfoot)*

In chapter six we find the balance, so as not to overload
the simple believer:

*"For if thou art able to bear the whole yoke of the lord, thou
shalt be perfect, but if thou art not able, do that which thou art
able". (Didache 6- Lightfoot)*

Another widely known early Christian writing was the
Epistle to Diognetus. Several passages (often cited in history
books) show us a style of life very much in line with the Gospels.

*"For the Christians are distinguished from other men nei-
ther by country, nor language, nor the customs which they observe. For they neither inhabit cities of their own, nor employ a
peculiar form of speech, nor lead a life which is marked out by
any singularity. The course of conduct which they follow has not
been devised by any speculation or deliberation of inquisitive
men; nor do they, like some, proclaim themselves the advocates
of any merely human doctrines. But, inhabiting Greek as well
as barbarian cities, according as the lot of each of them has
determined, and following the customs of the natives in respect*

to clothing, food, and the rest of their ordinary conduct, they display to us their wonderful and confessedly striking method of life. They dwell in their own countries, but simply as sojourners. As citizens, they share in all things with others, and yet endure all things as if foreigners. Every foreign land is to them as their native country, and every land of their birth as a land of strangers. They marry, as do all [others]; they beget children; but they do not destroy their offspring. They have a common table, but not a common bed. They are in the flesh, but they do not live after the flesh. They pass their days on earth, but they are citizens of heaven. They obey the prescribed laws, and at the same time surpass the laws by their lives. They love all men, and are persecuted by all. They are unknown and condemned; they are put to death, and restored to life. They are poor, yet make many rich; they are in lack of all things, and yet abound in all; they are dishonored, and yet in their very dishonor are glorified. They are evil spoken of, and yet are justified; they are reviled, and bless; they are insulted, and repay the insult with honour; they do good, yet are punished as evil-doers. When punished, they rejoice as if quickened into life; they are assailed by the Jews as foreigners, and are persecuted by the Greeks; yet those who hate them are unable to assign any reason for their hatred." (Epistle to Diognetus 5. ANF of 1885 p26-27 also Master Christian Library 2000 by Ages)

The early Church was a different breed. Though they early mixed our Lord's teachings with Platonism, nevertheless the world got a look at truth in living flesh. The kind of virtue that the philosophers could only speculate on was put on display in the transformed lives and hearts of people who had met Jesus Christ and not only wanted salvation, but they wanted Jesus living within them. The words of the letter quoted above are just ideas until they are believed, and they are only abstract beliefs until they are acted upon. Though it's true that Christians of today must decry the attempt of modern critics to find the "historical Jesus" when He is faithfully and consistently presented before us in the most amazing biographical testimonies of ancient literature, we wind up looking not for the historical Jesus, but wondering why Christians believe almost nothing that the historical Jesus was, nor much of anything that He said. Protestants must face the fact that they have turned Jesus into an icon as surely as any Orthodox or Catholic has. We present the world with a crucifix as surely as any Catholic. To be sure, it is not a pictorial one, but a historical one. We present the world with a creed to be accepted, not a living statement of Christ in its face to challenge the core of godless materialism. The early Church had the real Jesus, just like much of the persecuted Church has today.

Unfortunately the teachings of Jesus got thoroughly mixed in with Stoicism, and everything got mixed in with Platonism (the teachings of the philosopher Plato) so that what came out was an ascetic distortion: people fleeing to the monastery to become holy. Not what Jesus taught. Poverty, obedience and chastity - again, not quite what Jesus taught and not quite the way He taught it.

No greater demonstration of the transforming power of the words of Jesus could be found than the testimony of the early Church in becoming the dominant intellectual and spiritual force in the Roman Empire. Roman iron met **"Blessed are the meek"** and it turned out that the meek really did inherit the earth. The poor in spirit were thrown to the lions and the Church grew. When there was plague or epidemic, the Christians were there taking care of the sick, giving no regard to their own safety. (See the testimony of that in Eusebius). Their testimony was a shining light that drew literally millions to Jesus.

Unfortunately the temper of the times drew out a false, self-seeking attitude toward poverty, obedience and chastity that bore fruit in a convoluted view of the New Testament. Jesus had said that the persecuted were blessed; nowhere had He said that their bones were blessed. Nowhere had He said that their bones had the power to bless others. Nevertheless, God allowed that Church to grow even in the midst of a distortion: making a work of the flesh out of the Christian virtues. In the save way God blesses the Church today even in the midst of a distortion: reducing the truth to a "Gospel of Grace" that precludes any living expression of that grace in the Body of Christ. This current distortion makes God the ultimate indulgence peddler and leaves this generation helpless against the secular juggernaut arrayed against it.

In any case, the blood of the martyrs was the seed of the Church. Our generation is afraid to trust that a people who embrace the Sermon on the Mount could be more effective as evangelists than the preachers. Yes, we have our soup kitchens - and we should - and we have our city rescue missions - and we should have them and support them - but Jesus said that all men would know we are His disciples by our love. The early Church tried it and it worked.

What was their plan of evangelism? "Blessed are the meek."

How is America going to be reached? How about, "Blessed are the poor in Spirit"? Or better yet, as in Luke, "Blessed are the poor." They had better results with that method in the early Church than the prosperity preachers with unbiblical teachings for the richest people on earth. Put some people out there who really love one another, whose love for one another overflows its banks and washes over those around them, and the conversions will come faster than the persecutors can kill them. It worked in ancient Rome. It is still working in much of Asia and Africa. China's church grew under persecution. In Russia, the babushkas just kept coming to the churches year after year, generation after generation, in spite of persecution and the fact that it was illegal for anyone to give them religious training. Nevertheless, they just kept coming. The Protestants grew too; nothing could hold them back because nothing could separate them from the love of God. Persecuted churches had to hang together and intertwine their lives. The Sermon on the Mount was fulfilled even though they were not necessarily trying to fulfill it, and when they started keeping the commands of Jesus- particularly the command to love one another - nothing could keep the Father away. But back to our story.

St Patrick was the first of a lot of monks coming out of Ireland (though he himself was originally from England). They read a lot of the Bible at face value. They certainly had distortions - let him that is without distortions cast the first stone - but it was not from them that the teachings of Jesus were put on the shelf to gather dust. From Ireland and England the monks fanned out all over Europe - Germany, France, the Low Countries, even Italy - spreading learning and the Gospel as they understood it. God blessed their endeavors; they are credited with having a lot to do with the conversion of Europe.

When St. Francis of Assisi came along half a millennium later, the church was in terrible shape. Many practices had come in that were outright against the work of God. Nevertheless, when St. Francis and some others started viewing life through the words of Jesus, God blessed even the Church in that age. St. Francis' discovery of the simple life, as taught by Jesus, even when filtered through a medieval ascetic lens, was a renewing, hope-building breath of fresh air for the multitudes. The fact that many tried to follow him, but without St. Francis' obedience to the words of Jesus, and wound up creating an institution that even St. Francis abhorred was just proof that to those who keep the words of Jesus, God pours Himself out. To those who don't, He is much more sparing of His blessings. When the church deviates, then she has to go it on her own steam.

People who were greatly impacted by the teachings of Jesus have had major impact on the Church at critical times throughout Her history. Jesus' teachings are not idle words for idle monks. In reality, the monks were not idle: they built the roads, cleared the land, converted Europe, took in the orphans, developed agriculture, maintained learning, and a host of other things that are coming to light. All this was because they were guided by some level of Christ's teachings in the middle of a misguided church. They received a measure of blessing. In the midst of a church that did not believe in justification by faith, by faith they believed in Jesus and His words. This is certainly more than a lot of Evangelicals do today. Viewing it one way, monasticism institutionalized the teachings of the Sermon on the Mount, just like many of our modern outreach programs institutionalize evangelism - with destructive results.

With the Reformation came the restoration of the truth of justification by faith. This desperately needed breakthrough by Luther began to dissolve the centuries of ecclesiastical stranglehold on the life of the Church. People were set free from bondage to works, penance, veneration of images, etc. The story is well known.

Among those who were touched was a group that has come to be known as the Anabaptists. They reasoned that since we are set right with God through faith, then we have no business being baptized unless we are believers. This was logical enough, although Luther did not buy it. What is important about them is that there sprang up a people fully embracing the Sermon on the Mount at one of the bloodiest times in European history. Although practices varied from group to group, they lived at peace, even unto death. They eschewed wealth, fame, oaths, state churches, and a good many other things besides. The teachings of Jesus were their daily bread. Oh, and by the way. . . they found out that "**blessed are you when men shall persecute you.**" Thousands of them were hunted down by Catholics and Protestants alike, both equally guilty, both absolutely given over to the high priest's words, "We have no king but Caesar." Protestantism lost its divine sanction right there.

More than a little Anabaptist theology can be found in the Church today; witness the number of churches that practice believers' baptism. We certainly do not need to drive buggies and farm with horses, but the fact still remains that a people who take Jesus' words seriously can hang together in the face of the modern world. They can still maintain an identity. This bears testimony to the power of their original ideals founded on the teachings of Jesus.

The Moravians brought the gospel to the Indians of North America. The Moravians had some communal background, were more into the Sermon on the Mount than anyone around. Some of their missionaries converted the Wesleys and Whitefield. From this came the modern holiness movement, and revivalism of the 18th & 19th centuries. Much of the missionary movement and much of what is vital to the growth of

Christian outreach came out of Pietist/ Moravian roots. People who knew that there was a life to be lived in Christ and who had persevered into a depth of relationship with Jesus were empowered to reach out in ways that could transform lives even when the churches were dead.

Unfortunately, this is too short of a survey, but the main point is that what was vital and living in previous ages was a Christian faith that was totally different than much of the so called faith of our age, having much more in common with the faith as it is practiced in the under-developed world than it has with the stuff being heard in most churches in America. The previous generations served God with their lives as well as their lips- or at least believed they were supposed to.

In this part of the book we have endeavored to demonstrate the heavenly origin of Jesus' teachings: they come from the heart of the Father. They are spiritual words: they cannot be received by flesh. Jesus received these words and handed them on, and the Holy Spirit now gives the power for them to become life. In anything that God has done, these principles have been the goal of God's operation:

He has told you, O man, what is good;
And what does the LORD require of you
But to do justice, to love kindness,
And to walk humbly with your God? (Mic 6:8)

God's purpose was to send His Son to the Earth as the incarnate Word, have his Son choose twelve men to follow Him and be instructed in these teachings, and then the Son would lay down His life that there might be clean vessels filled with the Spirit of God who could disciple all nations in these principles.

How all of this goes awry is the subject of the next section of this book.

125

Part 2

Thy Will be Done on Earth

W E GO NOW TO THE biggest stumbling block facing Christians in the West: the religious mind. Perhaps the biggest difficulty here is that we all think that religiosity is one problem that we don't have, and never will have. This misconception will occupy much of the next part of this book, and we cannot give it short shrift because it is so prevalent and so deadly.

We are parts of a fragmented society on a race to the bottom. We have grown up in a broken church system that did not nurture us in anything godly, and we all face the particular challenges of DNA, family and circumstances.

For He rescued us from the domain of darkness, and transferred us to the kingdom of His beloved Son, in whom we have redemption, the forgiveness of sins. (Col 1:13&14)

The Blood of Jesus was spilled to redeem us out of every kingdom of this world into the kingdom of God's beloved Son. Unfortunately, many of the redeemed do not seem to want that kingdom. We were to be transformed by the renewing of our minds. We were led to the Lord with a view to being liberated from this generation. Unfortunately, Christians have shown themselves to be as infatuated with the world as the pagans.

The other problem is the propagation of theologies that consistently work to smooth over that infatuation with the world by telling believers that all there is to do is get saved and tell others. In the rush to ditch formality and all the other things that man has placed between the individual and Jesus, much of the Christian world has ditched the Christian life. This is the one thing that the Church should present to the world. If the world saw a truly functioning Church it would marvel. In the self-conscious effort to strip out all religiosity from the church, believers merely wind up taking religiosity out of its stained glass environment and reducing it to a form that is comfortable in a living room or basement.

We will begin our study of the modern Christian mind with its chief actor, the Modern Pharisee.

9

THE MODERN PHARISEE

THERE IS PROBABLY NOTHING THAT modern Christians love to hate more than the ancient Jewish Pharisees. All decked out in their self - righteousness, opposed by no less than the Lord Himself, the valiant defenders of all that Jesus came to undo, who could deny 21st century Christians the right to go after the Pharisees? There they were, proudly trying to trap Jesus in His own words, intent on halting the spread of the gospel, the very picture of religiosity - certainly we have nothing in common with these 1st century bigots.

The modern church has made a cottage industry of shedding any vestiges of "religion." The very word is likely to bring a scowl out of contemporary believers. "Me? Religious? Hah!" We and the *philosophes* of the Enlightenment are comrades in arms against anything that smacks of "religion." Certainly when the world tries to label us as religious, we set the record straight that faith in Christ is not "religion."

In this battle against religion we call in Jesus, always portrayed as an anti-establishment figure, opposing the temple priesthood because of its slavish bondage to the Law of Moses. Certainly Jesus wasn't religious! We think of Him as the One who would change the laws, abolish the customs, do away with the temple, and usher in a new kingdom by force. . . Oddly enough, this analysis of Christ, so often put forth by the modern world, doesn't differ materially from what the Pharisees themselves thought of Jesus. They certainly thought of Jesus as a revolutionary character, intent on veering far from the faith of the fathers, tearing down everything in His path. His refusal to resist didn't quite fit into any of their categories - since they really didn't have many categories to fit people into - but they were sure that underneath He was a troublemaker and just wanting to stir things up.

As one reads the words of Jesus in scripture, there should come an uneasiness about all our smug modern wisdom, our clear vision twenty centuries later; our vaunted fidelity to our Lord's opposition to religion. The Law was brought to its end by fulfillment, and who could fulfill it better than Christ? Who better to end the "Thou shalt nots" than the One in whom all the promises of God find their "Yes?" In what way did Jesus undo the law? Let's look at a few laws.

"**Thou shalt not kill**" (Ex 20:13AV) This law was not abolished, its scope was increased logarithmically by the statement "**everyone who is angry with his brother. . .**" (Mt 5:22)

"**Thou shalt not commit adultery**" (Ex20:14 AV) was not done away with, its import was ratcheted up with the statement, "**Everyone who looks at a woman with lust for her. . .**" (Mt 5:28)

"**Thou shalt not steal**"(Ex 20:15AV) and "**Thou shalt not covet**" (Ex 20:17AV) are totally subsumed in the statement, "**Do** not worry about tomorrow. . . ." (Mt 6:34) A statement of the Law that is at least distantly possible for a human being is transformed into a proclamation that is possible only for a heavenly being - or at least someone full of the Holy Spirit.

The tithe is replaced with, "**Give, and it shall be given unto you.**" (Lk 6:38 AV)

If we read the scriptures carefully, we don't see Jesus abandoning the Law as such, we see Him beginning with the commandment and then launching out after the heart that gave the Law. Jesus went to the Father, the very fountainhead of the Law, and then went in pursuit of the very purpose for which the Law was given: the higher righteousness - the righteousness of God. Our Lord saw the mind of the Father in every page of the Law, and yet everywhere He went in Israel He saw lost humanity twisting those words for selfish purposes: Pharisees harping on morality while they themselves were moneygrubbers; the priests using the tithe to live sumptuously, using their status to ingratiate themselves with the Romans while the common people were innocently supporting it all with the offerings that the Law commanded. The poor widow whom Jesus commended for putting her last two mites into the temple treasury was actually supporting the corrupt religious establishment that killed Jesus a short time later. She didn't know it then but Jesus did, and He commended her for her action because she was, in her heart, fulfilling the intent of the Law. Because she was doing it in faith, she also became one of the heirs of God by faith.

The Old Testament Pharisee was in the Temple showing the world how righteous he was. He was openly putting his money into the treasury to show his generosity, he was standing around making great swelling prayers, showing that he was a man of God, certainly a cut or two above that publican over there. The modern Pharisee is not impressed.

The modern Pharisee is not in the church boasting about how religious he is, he's in church - or in someone's living room - demonstrating how religious he isn't. He doesn't boast about his tithing- that would be Old Testament- he boasts about how he doesn't tithe at all. He doesn't boast about his generosity to the poor - no social gospel for him! Big car, big house, obviously the favored of God! Judgmental? Not the modern Pharisee! Why

Jesus has set me free,
So I won't judge you
If you won't judge me!

The Old Testament Pharisee knew he was righteous only on the basis of works that he did. The Modern Pharisee reckons himself righteous - and especially beloved of God - because he has no works.

Now, in reality, neither one has anything to do with the righteousness of God which is by faith. Neither one accords with Biblical truth, whether Old Testament or New Testament.

Even with the intent of God plainly laid out in the New Testament, we still see the Pharisees' old game being played out in the church of our day; but of course the clothing is modern. The Pharisee of old stood in the temple, declaring unto God his righteousness, "I tithe ten percent of all that I get. I fast twice a week. I give alms." This is certainly not the prayer of the modern Pharisee, but the heart is strangely similar in his prayer, "Oh God, I know you hear me. I don't tithe, I don't give unless you really tell me to. I hardly pray. I despise tradition, religion, form and authority. Hear me since I am not religious. Oh yes - please give me lots of money."

132

The modern Pharisee is as much a child of religious works as the old Pharisee was; he has not abolished religiosity, he has merely redefined it, making it amenable to twenty-first century sensitivities. The old way of the Pharisees we know to be religiosity. Let's call the modern way "irreligiosity."

The old way justified itself by its keeping of the Law; irreligiosity seeks its justification by the fact that it doesn't keep the Law - any law. No legalism, no dos and don'ts, and 70 in a 55 mile per hour zone to boot. Religiosity was certainly the child of righteousness because of what it did; irreligiosity is certain to stand among the righteous because it has nothing to show for its service unto God. It has not justified itself, it hasn't done works, it hasn't fed the poor or cared for the orphan and the widow. Therefore it must be depending on God's grace, right? And that must be faith - right? Therefore it stands in the church (or on the TV screen) proclaiming itself an heir of Jesus Christ, an heir of the grace of God.

All of this has no more to do with justification by faith than the indulgence sellers. The empty self-unrighteousness of the 20th century is as far afield as relics, images, and is just as works centered. Tetzel sold an indulgence which was little more than a license to sin; we have turned grace into a treasury of merit with unlimited drawing rights and no responsibility. In so doing we strip grace of the power to effectively do its work. Much of the modern church has so little to show for its faith because its faith is unreal. Since obviously (at least to the modern Pharisee) whatsoever is not of works is of faith, and whatsoever is not of faith is sin, the modern Pharisee is a unique creature in the history of religion: sin can become righteousness; we follow the world, the flesh and the devil because that is being not religious. The bottom line which is common to us and the Pharisees, to the old religiosity and new irreligiosity, is that both parties have exercised an unshakable faith in themselves, an overweening assurance that they are divinely favored, and an inordinate love of money. All of that leaves no room for God.

The Mind of the modern Pharisee and Questions That Lie

The Pharisee of today, as with the Pharisee of yesteryear, is all about lines and limits.

As we saw with the Parable of the Prodigal Son, the question, "Who is my neighbor?" is all about the line and the limit: who do I have to love, and who do I not have to love? What will happen to me if I don't love my neighbor?

"Is it lawful to give to Caesar or not?"

"Stone her or not?"

"Whose wife will she be? Pick a number from one to seven."

"Who gave you this authority?"

Always a straightforward choice: this or that, yes or no. The Pharisee stays on the good side of God's word, always able to justify himself, always able to assure himself that he is in good shape. The Pharisee is a creature of simple certainties: certain of his rightness according to the Bible, certain that God is pleased with him. The Pharisee of old did this through the Law; the modern Pharisee has met the requirements for salvation, prayed the prayer, and nothing can shake him from his assurance that God has appointed an extra legion of angels just for him. Because of this mindset, questions are simple and straightforward with clear choices. After all - the Pharisee knows that truth is black and white, and he is certain that God has given us simple tools to detect the difference.

But even a straightforward question cannot come from the Pharisaical mind without becoming a lethal weapon. This is the mind of fallen man. On the other hand, try these questions:

"Who do men say I am? Who do you say I am?"

"John's baptism- is it from heaven or from men?"

"Why do you seek the living among the dead?"

"Is it lawful to do good on the Sabbath, or to do evil?"

"Peter, do you love (*agape*) me?"

"A man had two sons. . . Which one did the will of his father?"

These questions reveal the thoughts and intentions of the heart and shed light on the condition of the hearer. They define us in our relationship to God.

Now try the questions of this age:

"Do I have to forgive my brother in order for God to forgive me?"

"I've accepted Jesus; what happens if I just go my own way and have a good time?"

"Can I kill somebody and still belong to the Lord?"

The endless questions of, "Where is the line" or more appropriately, "What is the exact requirement?"

Now, just as a thought experiment, let's try these questions out for size:

"If I run around with other women, am I still married to you?

"Do I have to love my wife?"

"Dad, if I shoot up the school, will you still love me?"

"Dad, will you still love me if I curse you? Will you love me just as I am?"

We are far more comfortable trying out our godless questions on God than we are in trying them out on others who we can see. We are even more uncomfortable trying them out on ourselves

All of us have, after coming to the Lord, degraded the name of our Savior. Graciously we have all received forgiveness. We have not begun to plumb the depths of His great mercy; we don't have to kill somebody to do so. We do not have to sin for grace to abound; a people walking in the light will do a much better job of showing forth God's grace than an army of reformed drug addicts who have been turned into middle-class Americans. Grace reigns through righteousness unto eternal life; it does not multiply through carnality.

When the chief priests and elders asked Jesus about the source of His authority, Jesus refused to take up the question because the question was a lie. We have always thought that questions were neutral and that there was always a yes or no answer, but questions are more subtle liars than statements. Questions define the territory; they measure out the field of argument.

When He entered the temple, the chief priests and the elders of the people came to Him while He was teaching, and said, "By what authority are You doing these things, and who gave You this authority?" (Mt 21:23)

When they ask where Jesus' authority came from, they did not want to know any such thing: they wanted to stone Him. When Jesus responded with a question,

"The baptism of John was from what source, from heaven or from men?" And they began reasoning among themselves, saying, "If we say, 'From heaven,' He will say to us, 'Then why did you not believe him?'" (Mt 21:25)

He was revealing the true territory: those Pharisees had no clue about Divine authority. They were not under Divine authority and couldn't recognize it. If Jesus answered their question He would have put Himself in a position where they would put Him (bodily) under their authority. The Son of God had no business putting Himself under the authority of the perverse, and He knew it. When we play their games we come under their authority. When we let them draw the lines and define the issues we leave no room for the authority of God. Since their question obscured the truth, why should Jesus reveal His authority to them? He could not reveal anything to them.

Is it lawful to pay tax to Caesar or not?

This question is a lie because it presents a context in which truth cannot live. God is not confined to our "either-ors". When both answers to a question yield a false answer the question is a lie.

Most of the questions we ask God are lies, as are many of the questions that occupy the church.

Is there eternal security?

Well, you tell the saints that are following God in the midst of trial and persecution that they are in God's hands and no one can pluck them out. You tell the miracle-working preachers on our church platforms and TV screens that they are two-fold more the children of hell then the drug peddlers and the whores, and that unless they repent they are going to face damnation. For those in the middle, there is the wisdom of God and a balanced presentation of the word of God.

Perhaps to understand better that questions can be liars, we need to look at the biblical understanding of lying.

When the Ten Commandments were given, God did not say, "Thou shalt not lie." What He said was, "**Thou shalt not** bear false witness." There is a big difference. If I take facts and use them to point in the wrong direction, I may be able to convince myself that I am not lying, but I will not be able to convince anybody that I am not bearing false witness. When we testify to error we are liars, even if all the details are true. When we selectively use true statements to cover a twisted heart, we may not be "lying", but we are giving a false witness. God is all about heart, God is all about meaning; anything to obscure the true heart is a false witness, even if it is not, upon inspection, a lie.

When my question leads the flow of truth astray it is a lie. When my interrogation convicts the innocent, I have lied, regardless of the technicalities of definition, and even if I have made no statements, only questions.

The modern Pharisee, like the Pharisee of old, is a creature of false dilemmas: "Is this sin?" "What's wrong with. . .?" "Do I have to?" The modern Pharisee is on the other side of the coin than the Old Testament Pharisee was, but like Caesar's coin, it has no place in the temple. It does not fit.

We could not picture the Son of God asking, "Father, do I have to serve You?" "Father, will you love me even if. . .?"

God has given us the power to love, the power to embrace the things of God. We prove out the grace of God far more in our confused efforts to serve Him, our twisted attempts to love the brethren, and go the extra mile, than we do when we give our testimony for the forty-third time. We find the essence of the heart that saved us each time we fall short of that grace in our walk of faith.

We test the lines and the limits because we are not searching out the Heart that gave the word. Even more so, we test the lines and the limits because we are creatures of the knowledge of good and evil. By this knowledge, originally forbidden by God, we become the pilots of our own lives. No longer directed by the voice of God, through it we have inner knowledge of what to do. By it we judge all things. By the knowledge of good and evil many of the proud stand in their own boastfulness proclaiming, as did their ancient counterparts, how righteous they are and how sad they are that so many others are not. We become pop existentialists, creating our own reality, living in it, and judging the world by it.

The biblical testimony to salvation is not whether we have said a certain prayer or acknowledged a certain set of facts, the biblical testimony is the presence and operation of the Holy Spirit in the life. Paul in Galatians:

This is the only thing I want to find out from you: did you receive the Spirit by the works of the Law, or by hearing with faith? (Ga 3:2)

That is the issue: the source of the presence of the Holy Spirit.

The one who keeps His commandments abides in Him, and He in him. We know by this that He abides in us, by the Spirit whom He has given us. (1Jn 3:24)

The Spirit is the proof that God is in us. What that verse says about the commandments also speaks for itself. The fact that it is coupled by John with the reference to the Spirit tells us that all of this is for this age, not the next. The modern Pharisee's certainties put him in a lonely position, but he'll never notice it.

Having seen that questions can lie, we must also realize that truth is not always what it seems. Several times in the Gospels Jesus rebukes a spirit for announcing that Jesus is the Holy One of God:

saying, "What business do we have with each other, Jesus of Nazareth? Have You come to destroy us? I know who You are - the Holy One of God!" (Mk 1:24)

"Let us alone! What business do we have with each other, Jesus of Nazareth? Have You come to destroy us? I know who You are - the Holy One of God!" (Lu 4:34)

Jesus was not impressed with all of this.

And Jesus rebuked him, saying, "Be quiet, and come out of him!" (Mk 1:25)

But Jesus rebuked him, saying, "Be quiet and come out of him!" And when the demon had thrown him down in the midst of the people, he came out of him without doing him any harm. (Lk 4:35)

If Jesus' only goal was that His position as the Messiah should be announced, then it is puzzling that He would shut the demons up. This was supernatural testimony to His lordship. However, the truth is that uncleanness cannot proclaim a holy God. Demons cannot take even that most vital of truths and bear witness to Jesus; only truth can do that. Only those who have surrendered to Him can do that. That is why so many preachers go wrong: they are unholy vessels monkeying with holy things. It has been that way for centuries, and the Catholic Church did a good job of handing it on to Protestants. Truth bears witness to truth; ambition cannot get there, greed and envy cannot do it.

Now it is true that Paul said:

Some, to be sure, are preaching Christ even from envy and strife, but some also from good will; the latter do it out of love, knowing that I am appointed for the defense of the gospel; the former proclaim Christ out of selfish ambition rather than from pure motives, thinking to cause me distress in my imprisonment.

What then? Only that in every way, whether in pretense or in truth, Christ is proclaimed; and in this I rejoice.

Yes, and I will rejoice, (Php 1:15-18)

It is true that God will bless His sheep: God will protect His sheep from envy and strife, and God will make all things work together for good to those that love Him. This is absolutely true. But God never intended envy and strife to proclaim the lordship of the Prince of Peace. God never intended greed and avarice to proclaim the Lamb who gave everything that we might be saved. Although this has been going on for two thousand years, the fruits of the envy and strife are everywhere, so much so that much of the witness is false. Just as the demons were not doing Jesus a service by shouting out, so many of our outreach efforts are doing harm, as are many of our churches, as are many of our broadcasts. God is not served when I wrap my ambition around a truth: Jesus died so that His holiness could be proclaimed by clean vessels.

For a little more understanding of the problem we are going to tell a story - total fiction.

One day little Suzie Q was playing with her big brother's blocks. When her mother came in a few minutes later five of the blocks said

E = mc 2 (The 2 was a little bit up from the c.)

To Suzie's mother it was obvious that there was a genius in the family: her little girl had independently reasoned out a significant corollary from Einstein's theory of relativity.

Now to the rest of the world this was nothing: just a very curious accident by a toddler.

None of us would reckon that she was a scientific genius, ready to go forth into quantum physics. She did not know what "E" stood for, nor "m", nor "c", nor for that matter, "2," but here it was, the most famous formula in physics. Any reasonable person would say that this incident means nothing. Why? Because we all recognize that statements are not meaningful when separated from their truth systems. And just as the little girl cannot produce advanced physics, Jesus's lordship cannot be proclaimed by demons or corrupt preachers because they are separated from all elements of the truth of that kind of a statement.

On the other hand, when little Suzie Q goes around the house singing, "Jesus loves me," biblically she is spot-on: this is the real deal. Why? Because a child has the whole system of faith that an adult only strives to have. When a politician tells a conservative electorate that he believes Jesus died for his sins nobody is impressed. The words are all correct, but even the preachers of cheap grace don't praise God that we have another believer. The truth system that that kind of truth lives in simply does not exist in that politician, nor does he dwell in it. All truth lives in an environment, and apart from that environment is simply a bumper sticker. The Gospel is the power of God unto salvation when it is proclaimed by a living believer. It is merely another competing advertisement when it is in the hands of an unbelieving church and just panders to consumers. Love, true love, is the driving power of truth and knowledge. When Paul says,

And this I pray, that your love may abound still more and more in real knowledge and all discernment, so that you may approve the things that are excellent, in order to be sincere and blameless until the day of Christ; (Php 1:9&10)

He shows us where knowledge, the knowledge of God, comes from: it abounds from love.

For I want you to know how great a struggle I have on your behalf and for those who are at Laodicea, and for all those who

have not personally seen my face, that their hearts may be encouraged, having been knit together in love, and attaining to all the wealth that comes from the full assurance of understanding, resulting in a true knowledge of God's mystery, that is, Christ Himself, (Col 2:1&2)

Again Paul puts love into the equation about knowledge. If we had a Church knit together by love we would have what he speaks of in another place

that He would grant you, according to the riches of His glory, to be strengthened with power through His Spirit in the inner man, so that Christ may dwell in your hearts through faith; and that you, being rooted and grounded in love, may be able to comprehend with all the saints what is the breadth and length and height and depth, and to know the love of Christ which surpasses knowledge, that you may be filled up to all the fullness of God. (Eph 3:16–19)

Love is everywhere, and the knowledge of God follows love. And the practical aspects of that love are nowhere more clearly laid out than in the teachings of Jesus. As those words live in the heart, God lives in the life, God lives in the praises, God lives in the words spoken, and God is resident in the thoughts of that heart.

The one who does not love does not know God, for God is love. (1Jn 4:8)

The reason the world does not take the Church seriously is because the church has not taken God seriously. Where there is a living Church that takes God seriously then the world has a powerful force to reckon with. Paul speaks of faith, hope, and love: this is the truth system from which valid statements about God come. Apart from that, we are like children playing with blocks and shouting triumphantly when they come together.

Jesus said that we must become like little children in order to enter the kingdom (Mt 18:3). The reason is that only a child can learn a language without a foreign accent. Only a child can speak the language that God speaks. The rest of us must learn about the heavenly things just like adults learn a foreign language: work books and grammar, heavy instruction, and we still wind up with a telltale accent. Theology is Truth as a Foreign Language. The child is able to speak as one native born. Thus we must be born again: we must start over and learn the definition of all words from the mouth of God, their proper usage, etc. This can only be done in the environment in which God still speaks: the living Church. The Church in China can be a living witness to the power of God in the midst of persecution whereas the church in America struggles to give her own children anything more to live for than a good job and heaven someday. Truth does not live in a system like that. People go to seminary to learn God's vocabulary and still they talk like an off shore-answering service: the message is not comprehendible to the ones that are supposed to hear it.

Many people talk about Christ, many say things about "grace", "salvation", etc. All these are words they have learned from the books or from theologians. The only way to accurately learn about them is to be taught them by God. Jesus is the dictionary that defines all terms. His words as recorded in the Bible are the witness to every word that proceeds from the heart of God.

The words of the LORD are pure words;

As silver tried in a furnace on the earth, refined seven times. (Ps 12:6)

So the question arises: are Christians under the law? The short answer is "no." The long answer is that the question is a lie: it assumes that all Christians are in the same condition, and what on earth we mean by "the law" I'll never know. If Jesus Christ is living in me and I am abiding in Him then I am above all rule and authority, seated with Christ. If I am enslaved to my flesh, then maybe the preacher will tell me, on the supposed authority of Paul, that I am not "under"

"Thou shalt not steal" (Ex 20:15 AV)

but presumably, on the authority of Paul, I am under

He who steals must steal no longer; but rather he must labor, performing with his own hands what is good, so that he will have something to share with one who has need. . . (Eph 4:28)

I am not sure what the difference is between **"Thou shalt not steal"** and **"He. . . must steal no longer."** Paul could tell me the most sweeping things about my liberty in Christ, but Paul spoke as a bond-slave of Jesus Christ, and in that position he was the freest of men. He did not tell them in practical exhortations about their freedom from restraint; he told them what the Spirit of God was telling him to tell them, and if it sounded a bit Old Testament, then so be it. Paul could offer a sacrifice because he was not under the Law but under grace. He could keep the Sabbath because he was not under the Law but under grace just like he could eat with Gentiles because he was not under the Law but under grace.

It is a seldom observed fact that Paul, whose gospel sets us free from the law, describes the antichrist as the "Lawless One." Paul, who was not under the Law of Moses, but rather under the Law of Christ, describes the prevailing demonic spirit of the last days in these terms:

For the mystery of lawlessness is already at work; only he who now restrains will do so until he is taken out of the way. Then that lawless one will be revealed whom the Lord will slay with

the breath of His mouth and bring to an end by the appearance of His coming; (2Th 2:7&8)

Notice that "lawlessness" is not a pretty term coming from the apostle who proclaimed our freedom from law. "The lawless one" is not a term for a saint. Anarchy is anarchy whether they say they believe in Jesus or not. The 21st century craving for untrammeled freedom is seen to be alien to the gospel, alien to Christian liberty, and alien to the purposes of God. "Give me liberty or give me death," is not the saying of a saint, however useful it may have been at a particular point of American history. "Don't tread on me" is the last cry of the serpent, not the saint- just look at that flag. **"For to me, to live is Christ and to die is gain" (Php1:21)** is the saying of a saint. Such a person can never be bound, and such a person fulfills the Law in all things.

Much of what is preached about freedom and liberty, especially in America, is nothing other than the spirit of lawlessness that Paul claimed would be the hallmark of the final apostasy. Many of the people running around are not telling about their freedom from the Law of Moses, but rather are proclaiming their independence from the Law of Christ

To the Jews I became as a Jew, so that I might win Jews; to those who are under the Law, as under the Law though not being myself under the Law, so that I might win those who are under the Law; to those who are without law, as without law, though not being without the law of God but under the law of Christ, so that I might win those who are without law. (1Co 9: 20&21)

Bear one another's burdens, and thereby fulfill the law of Christ. (Ga 6:2)

If Christ has set us free from the Law then we should be living and walking under grace. If we are not actively functioning under grace, and if we are not under the Law either, then we are lawless.

For the grace of God has appeared, bringing salvation to all men, instructing us to deny ungodliness and worldly desires and to live sensibly, righteously and godly in the present age, looking for the blessed hope and the appearing of the glory of our great God and Savior, Christ Jesus, who gave Himself for us to redeem us from every lawless deed, and to purify for Himself a people for His own possession, zealous for good deeds.

These things speak and exhort and reprove with all authority. Let no one disregard you. (Titus 2:11-15)

Needless to say, there are many churches where this kind of grace- Paul's kind of grace – is unheard of. Many people fuss about "the Law" when what they really are really objecting to is discipline. Grace is an operative power in which we come under the government of God for the fulfillment of His purposes.

For our proud confidence is this: the testimony of our conscience, that in holiness and godly sincerity, not in fleshly wisdom but in the grace of God, we have conducted ourselves in the world, and especially toward you. (1Cor 2:12)

We can see from this that Paul's grace was not an obnoxious form of "liberty" whereby he would thumb his nose at people and then mutter, "I'm under grace." It was not the moral vacuum that fills our suburban churches whereby Christians can cheat on taxes, be bigoted, live in a mindset of greed, and then throw stones at the world for being the ones to do something about the poor, about discrimination, and about the plundering of God's creation. The only tool the world knows is government and they aren't afraid to use it. Our only tool is the Holy Spirit and we live in gross ignorance of His power and His purposes.

Lawlessness is the foundation of much of what is preached in many of our churches these days, and it is the singular hallmark of the decay of the last days. We desperately need to read Paul and take seriously what he said, instead of overlaying upon him a bunch of theological ideas that simply do not fit into the spiritual world that his writings portray.

A Final Note about the Modern Pharisee

Many people will read this book and say that the objective of it is that we keep the Sermon on the Mount. The Modern Pharisee will still ask, "Do I have to keep the Sermon on the Mount or not?" That mindset cannot keep the Sermon on the Mount. That mindset will turn it into a law; it can do nothing else. This is what drives the godlessness of our churches- we either have holiness drilled until people literally have to flee, or we have this "grace" (which I would call "disgrace") that shoves the Holy Spirit out in the dark since Jesus did everything 2000 years ago.

If you have come out of a legalistic religious setting, there is very little you can do towards true holiness until that hammer of religious "holiness" that was placed over your head is removed. Until you can move with freedom and enjoy the liberty that truly is in Christ, just revel in liberty. We are not referring to you when we talk about the cheap grace peddlers. You need to find a place that proclaims the liberty that we have in Christ and start walking until you are free- and you won't be under the Law.

For others who have grown up in the freewheeling culture of our day, the words of the indulgence peddlers are going to be as deadly as any legalistic nonsense that has ever been proclaimed in the name of holiness. Paul admitted to the deadliness of law: the letters in stone murdered him. However, according to Paul it is not just the Law that kills, it is the letter that kills, and we have a culture of preachers who fill our television screens and murder people by the million. They take the tablets of stone and hammer out a graven image of G-R-A-C-E and make it as deadly and as far from Christ as the ancient Pharisees did with the Law. These people are free from the Law but not under the leadership of the Spirit.

But may it never be that I would boast, except in the cross of our Lord Jesus Christ, through which the world has been crucified to me, and I to the world. For neither is circumcision anything, nor uncircumcision, but a new creation. And those who will walk by this rule, peace and mercy be upon them, and upon the Israel of God.

From now on let no one cause trouble for me, for I bear on my body the brand-marks of Jesus. (Ga 16:14-17)

10

THE LITERAL TRUTH

ONE OF THE FUNDAMENTAL TENETS of fundamentalism is biblical literalism. The idea is something like this: the Bible is to be taken literally if at all possible. If the passage is obviously figurative, then the literal meaning of the figure is to be sought.

I am no enemy of believing the Bible; in fact, I think I believe more of the Bible literally than anyone I know. I try to keep it that way. However, I am under no illusions about the matter: believing the Bible is no easy task. People toss off their belief in seven literal days of creation - I don't know. People tell me about how the temple is going to be rebuilt in Jerusalem - I don't know. People tell me how we will get 666 stamped on our foreheads- I don't know, but I don't think so. Some even say that, on the basis of the literal meaning of scripture, that Babylon will be rebuilt, when the fact of the matter is that Babylon is all around us.

It is easier to be very literal about the distant past and the far away future than to allow the biblical teaching to touch today. When Jesus says that except we become as little children we cannot enter the kingdom of God, I don't believe that literally. However, I know that the overwhelming majority of Bible believing people do not believe it at all. Some of them are on the television, professing their certainty of the Bible's truth, yet demonstrating their unbelief to any and all. Our younger generation, looking for something to believe in, isn't going to give that the time of day; many of them who grew up in the church saw that kind of parade every Sunday and opted out.

Christians like to think of themselves as people of the Book. The literal truths of the Bible are defended, the sanctity of the work is upheld, and the church of today is doing its job. All over the place - even in the letters to the editor - we see evolution by natural selection opposed and Bible believing Christians denouncing the secular humanism of our age. We see homeschooling abounding in order to provide an environment that is safe for our offspring, free from the meddling interference - or invasion - of the non-Christian world. Been there done that. Social activism attempts to uphold the word of God in the public forum, and reserve space for the Christian viewpoint in the debates that shape legislation and public opinion. Christian colleges labor to turn out young people who will be faithful to truth and oppose the encroachments of heathen scholarship. These things are undertaken as sincere responses generated from our understanding of the Bible, which means what it says and says what it means in plain language that anyone can understand.

This is well and good. Unfortunately, as the world has already figured out, not all of this is what is seems. Although the liberal establishment dumped the literal word of God for a house of cards built on imaginary ur-texts and "Q" document sources, the Bible believing crowd mythologized the literal word of God with dispensations, non-New Testament teachings about the ages (the Age of the Law, the Age of Grace, the age of the kingdom) and a variety of gospels (the Gospel of the Kingdom, the Gospel of Grace, the Gospel for the Jews). The average heathen Bible scholar believes more of the Bible literally than the average Bible thumping preacher. Show me the Bible believing television preacher and I will show you someone for whom the Sermon on the Mount is of less importance than it is for a homeless atheist. The more they talk about the literal word of God and the verbal inspiration of the scripture, the more you may be sure that they don't believe a word of it. Like the Pharisees of old or the Jesuits of the sixteenth century, there are more caveats than applications, more exceptions than instances.

Ask the preacher if he believes that "**blessed are the poor.**" Ask the preacher about the dangers of riches. Ask the preacher about "**Give and it shall be given unto you.**" (Good words for the congregation and bad words for the preacher). Ask the conservative literalist about love and certainly he will tell you how he doesn't hate anybody. Ask the preacher about the operation of the Holy Spirit and three out of four will give you a history lesson. After all, "Those things were for the early Church." The gifts which are biblically spoken of as being without repentance are declared to be totally repented of by God, who gave them.

Just as with the Pharisees of old, the gnat is proven to be unpalatable and the camel to be delicious. Things that have been the hallmark of Christians for the last 2000 years are proclaimed to be irrelevant, or non-binding, or merely helpful suggestions for today.

I have often thought about writing a book entitled, "*100 Scriptures That Have No Meaning.*" Now, by "have no meaning," I do not mean that they are meaningless; not by any means. I mean that for the average believer many passages have been written out of the entire belief system in a way to make them foreign: to invalidate them. This was done in another fashion in the early 20th century by neo orthodoxy, when they used the vocabulary of scripture and just gave it another meaning; a form of Orwellian "new speak." Thus the resurrection was talked about, even the Resurrection of Jesus was talked about, but after all was said, one was not sure where the Body was. There was talk about Christ, but upon inspection there was ether or a vapor that was supposed to be venerated, but no one was seen to be home.

Bible believing Christians would repudiate all this, as they should, but literal unbelief has its own set of tricks. The current form within evangelical circles pushes scriptures back into the past or up into the future, all the while hoping for the immanent return of Christ who will ignore the last 2000 years and turn us into His kingdom. Or the scriptures are applied to the Jews; thus the teachings of Jesus apply to the Jewish remnant that will be on earth in the future. Or they are thought to be un- Pauline. Or they are just plain ignored. We have a mindset in the church in the West that will believe in the literal rebuilding of the temple, some even believing in the literal rebuilding of Babylon, but they cannot even believe in any meaningful way that we are being built into a temple for God to dwell in. "Surely God isn't going to join me to those Methodists over there." It is easier to believe something that has no application to the present than to grapple with incorporating eternal spiritual principles into our hearts and into our daily lives in the 21st century. Again it is easier to believe that there will be a mark on people's foreheads and hands than to believe that the carnal mind is enmity against God. It is easier to believe that there will be a seven headed monster coming out of the Mediterranean Sea near Tel Aviv than it is to see that the kingdoms of this world are already under the dominion of the evil one, and therefore we must live lives that do something about it - lives that redeem territory. The deluded fantasy of "taking America back for Jesus" assumes that America was His and that He wants it. He already said that His Kingdom was not of this earth. That is something we need to believe literally. But instead, we want to box His Kingdom into the confines of our territory, rather than leaving father and mother, leaving the territory that has imprisoned the word of God, and setting out for the land that God has given us.

Even the heathen Bible scholars believe that it is better to give than to receive; they just don't believe in a God who can bring it into reality, so it remains way out there. Christians believe in a God who can transform us by the renewing of our minds, but theology rattles around Christians' minds in a way that precludes allowing Him to do it. Anyway, "There probably isn't time." A thousand excuses. We nullify the word of God by our traditions and tomes of doctrine and centuries of accumulated unbelief. The unbelievers of the theology departments teach seminarians the transforming power of the dead letter because that is all that they know. Unfortunately, dead letter fails to transform hearts. The "Bible believers" in many of our churches don't even believe in the power of the living word, as applied by the Spirit of God. Oh yes, I forgot – it will save us so that we can go to heaven after we die. Show me that in the Bible and I will show you where it says, we are "**born again to a living hope through the resurrection of Jesus Christ from the dead,**" and again, "**the kingdom of heaven is at hand.**" We don't believe Jesus' opening statement 2,000 years later; we still see heaven as "out there." The Bible tells us that Jesus redeemed this earth, and we build our theologies on heaven. He sanctified us so that these bodies could bear His image, and we want to float around like cartoon saints of heaven - wings and all. Jesus told us to seek the true riches, which are in heaven, where we are seated with Christ at the right hand of God, and we want streets of gold somewhere beyond the blue, and plenty of gold here as well.

Show me our generation of Bible defending fundamentalists, busily running around the public arena defending Bible teachings on things that the world cannot, and will not relate to, and I'll show you a generation of Bible defending fundamentalists visibly denying in the public arena many very central biblical teachings that the world actually COULD relate to, and might, indeed, even pause to listen to.

Yes, believing the Bible is not easy. It requires a new birth. It requires the Holy Spirit.

As with all things of God there is a spiritual dynamic in the word of God that is preeminent. God is more interested that we not repeat the mistakes of Hezekiah than that we establish his dates within two months. Yet there really was a Hezekiah, and a Josiah, and an Adam and a Melchizedek. However, the scriptures are first and foremost the laying out of the heart of God. The historicity of them is part of what gives us the assurance that we, in fact, are building on truth. To make the historical foundations the roof and the walls is to create a structure that

God is not building. The Church is full of Christians who will defend to the death the seven literal day creation yet who do not in any way, shape, or form believe that God is their source, who do not believe in putting off the old man, putting to death their members which are upon the earth, etc. Totally reliant on the system, no different than the world around them, they are totally dependent on human resources: their savings, skills, education, connections, and position. But oh, yes, they are nevertheless convinced that God created everything in seven days - except their security. Oh yes, they are secure in heaven, just not right now. I guess God's right hand is not to extend this far or something. . . .

There is really no limit to what is not believed. We build whole theological systems on unbelief; our outlook is futuristic. Jesus said that if we had faith like a mustard seed we could move mountains. The issue at hand is not whether we can move mountains - we can hardly even move our own bodies, much less mountains. The issue is whether we will start down the road of faith, whether we will begin the process of believing, which means that we begin renouncing the elements of this age. We must be born again, all of us, each part of each believer. Now, not later; here, not there, just as the Bible says. God is not looking for people who will take the Bible literally; He is looking for people who will take the Bible seriously. He seeks those who will build their lives on the unseen realities of God's Kingdom, many of which are expressed in Jesus' teachings.

11

THE WORDS OF JESUS
AND THE DISPENSATIONS

THERE ARE SOME THINGS THAT are timeless. One never tires of natural wonders like the Grand Canyon or Niagara Falls; young and old will find them awe inspiring. Seeing a giant sequoia tree or a whale breaching can be an amazing experience for almost anybody. Perhaps it takes a train lover to appreciate the complexity and power of a big articulated steam locomotive, but although it may be obsolete, to the aficionados it is in the realm of the sublime. Let a fleet of tall ships come into a harbor and it makes the front page of the newspaper. Wine lovers like the old stuff - seemingly the older the better. Even in this fad-driven, live-for-today world there are some things that just cause us to pause and bask in the presence of the timeless. The human soul craves some sort of permanence, something that is not transitory.

Part of our coming to Jesus was out of that need: whether we came to Him out of our sense of alienation or out of our recognition of sin and separation from God, we needed to be joined to the Eternal; we needed an anchor, and we found Jesus Christ to be that anchor. God is unchanging. He is not subject to the vicissitudes of life, He is not subject to moods, nor can He be lobbied for His support for our favorite idea. He is not one way today and another way tomorrow. His steadfastness is the foundation on which we build.

"For I, the LORD, do not change; therefore you, O sons of Jacob, are not consumed. (Mal 3:6)

Jesus Christ is the same yesterday and today and forever. (Heb 13:8)

Every good thing given and every perfect gift is from above, coming down from the Father of lights, with whom there is no variation or shifting shadow. (Jas 1:17)

No shifting, no variation: steadfast.

Our modern society is built on philosophies of change. The concept of evolution and its adaptation by the popular culture starts working against the idea of permanence. We hear that, "Change is the only constant." That is a cute philosophy for a philosophy starved world, but it does not help the Church which is founded on bedrock. The philosophy of change wants to take the truth captive and bind it to today's ideas: the passing fad of the moment. The world fusses that the Church doesn't change enough, but the truth is that the world has changed the church too much already. We are established on the Creator of the laws of physics, the Creator of the elements in the periodic table, the Creator of the laws of mathematics. We don't need today's fad to help us along; we need deep roots in the God of Abraham, Isaac and Jacob, who swore an oath by Himself which started us on the road to salvation. We need to know the God Whose steadfast love never ceases, Whose word endures forever, Who spoke and it was. One expects that if God is constant like that, then He will honor His word. Words coming out of a steadfast person are not to be taken lightly. Whatever He says is not here today and gone tomorrow. If He says adultery is wrong today, it will be wrong tomorrow also. If today He says that covetousness is idolatry, then it will be tomorrow as well. If He says today that it is more blessed to give than to receive, then that will hold true for tomorrow as well. If today He says that we are to give expecting nothing in return, then we can trust that He will not say tomorrow, "Blessed are the tightwads." God's ordinances reflect values hidden in His heart and are indicative of the character of the Speaker. Now God may have said yesterday, "If you sin, slay a lamb," and today He says, "The Lamb has been slain, you need not slay one for yourselves." This is not indicative of change on the part of God - He has just introduced a more effective means to achieve His ends. The functional truth, **the wages of sin is death,** remains. Sin is still sin, requiring a radical solution, but now we know that, **the free gift of God is eternal life in Christ Jesus our Lord.** This was always true, for the Bible speaks of, **the Lamb slain before the foundation of the world;** (AV) it was done in the heart of God, fulfilled in the submission of the Son, but it just had not been revealed. The thought of God was revealed in Christ Jesus our Lord which is why He is called the Word.

Now that the gift of God has been revealed, it is still true that we are to give expecting nothing in return. The blood of Christ does not change God's attitude towards misers. The blood of Christ does not reverse the statement, **Blessed are the peacemakers,** and tilt the balance in favor of the war mongers.

Jesus' sacrifice has not changed the heart of God towards the proud and arrogant; it merely provides for the release from those sins that are abhorrent to the heart of God; a means of eradicating the sin nature (the old man) and installing a new government in the believer: the new man ruled by the Spirit of God. God's core values did not change; He whose mercies are new every morning, is still constant.

Dispensational teaching, while ostensibly upholding the constancy of God, tends to look at God's mode of government differently depending where in the time line we look. We hear of the "Church Age," "The Age of the Law," the Mosaic Dispensation," which is well and good; it is in fact true that:

God, after He spoke long ago to the fathers in the prophets in many portions and in many ways, in these last days has spoken to us in His Son, whom He appointed heir of all things, through whom also He made the world. (Heb 1:1&2)

God spoke in various ways - but His truth was the same whether it was said in Hebrew or Egyptian. The content did not vary whether it was said in Aramaic or in Greek. God was, in fact, introducing new modes of administration, and He was educating man to His eternal purposes. What was coming forth out of the mouth of God was the same whether He was speaking by a tabernacle, by parables, by prophets acting out elaborate mimes, by sovereign miracles, or by His Son,

And He is the radiance of His glory and the exact representation of His nature, and upholds all things by the word of His power. When He had made purification of sins, He sat down at the right hand of the Majesty on high, (Heb 1:3)

This truth, though elaborated in so many different ways, was the same in essence from generation to generation because it was locked up in the heart of the Father, the eternal, unchanging One. The Father spoke these things in these ways that His purpose might be revealed. God wanted this truth revealed and He made provision for its proclamation. Jesus in His very being was that provision, the living embodiment of the heart of the Father. He Himself was the dictionary that defined the basic terms of the life of the Father, which is the essence of the Kingdom of God. The Father's words were given to Jesus, Who alone could interpret them, and He passed them on to us according to the will of the Father.

for the words which You gave Me I have given to them; and they received them and truly understood that I came forth from You, and they believed that You sent Me. (Jn 17:8)

What Jesus was speaking was not just something for His day; what He was giving His disciples was not subject to the administrative "dispensation" that they happened to be under, and which, according to some, would come to an end shortly after Jesus' resurrection. Turning the other cheek was not a legal precept for the age when Jews would be on the earth and the Christians would be in heaven. It is a universal proclamation of the heart of the Father, retroactive to the beginning of time and good for eternity. When the Son of God was here He modeled it, and His injunction to us is that we should do as He did. We forsake all and follow Him because it's universal truth, and that's what He did in following the Father. The popular theology would have us believe that the Sermon on the Mount was given and then made irrelevant by the death of Jesus, or by the rejection of the Jews, or by whatever. It would have us believe that Jesus went to all the trouble to give out these words, even to the point of curtailing His public ministry so he had more time to teach His disciples, and then went to the cross so that we would have to wait until some other age for them to apply. Jesus said,

"Heaven and earth will pass away, but My words will not pass away". (Mt 24:35)

"Heaven and earth will pass away, but My words will not pass away". (Mk 13:31)

"Heaven and earth will pass away, but My words will not pass away". (Lk 21:33)

This means that no matter the dispensation, no matter the time, no matter what we think "God is doing right now," these words apply. The idea that these words are for the "Kingdom Dispensation" when the converted Jews would be here on the earth is put in question by the fact that Paul went out of his way to give Jesus' teachings to the Gentiles. He built his churches on them, he taught them, and he modeled his life on them. There is no future dispensation for the Jews because Christ crucified the difference between Jew and Gentile. Christ broke the barrier, there is one and only one entrance, or the totality of Paul's gospel is in ruins. He spoke of Jew and Gentile thus:

For He Himself is our peace, who made both groups into one and broke down the barrier of the dividing wall, by abolishing in His flesh the enmity, which is the Law of commandments contained in ordinances, so that in Himself He might make the two into one new man, thus establishing peace, (Eph 2:14&15)

For all of you who were baptized into Christ have clothed yourselves with Christ. There is neither Jew nor Greek, there is neither slave nor free man, there is neither male nor female; for you are all one in Christ Jesus. (Ga 3:27&28)

Even the distinctions of male and female don't survive the joining into Christ. Maybe that is why Jesus said:

Jesus said to them, "The sons of this age marry and are given in marriage, but those who are considered worthy to attain to that age and the resurrection from the dead, neither marry nor are given in marriage; for they cannot even die anymore, because they are like angels, and are sons of God, being sons of the resurrection. (Lk 20:34-36)

If we have evidence that not even marriage and male and female are making it into that kingdom (dispensation?), then are we to build systems of theology that separate Jew and Gentile with a wall of stone forever? Or for the Thousand Years? Or even for a day? Jews were Jews because they kept the Law, not by their birth. Any Jew who did not keep the Law was separated from the nation. That is Old Testament. Most of the people in Palestine with Israeli passports are not Jews by biblical standards. We have reason to believe that God is going to plead His case with them, but that is to join them to Christ, where there is neither Jew nor gentile.

Now, are we saying that God is going to tear up the Pentateuch and stick in the Sermon on the Mount? No, that is not the way truth works. God was taking down stone Laws and substituting the living Christ, and giving us His words as the testimony to what He looks like, and almost no theologians are listening. The church in the West does not look like Christ, nor is it described by His words. The world sees this with crystal clarity.

"One Door and only One." We all have our access, and all who are in Christ Jesus are the promised descendants of Abraham. Paul affirms that God will bring the Jewish nation in, but the whole Book tells us that they will go through the same Door as we all do. No dispensational outlook is allowed to put the teachings of our Lord in the background any more then they can put the Lord Jesus Christ in the background, because Jesus gave His life on Calvary to put His Person and His teachings in the foreground, with a new life, the Holy Spirit, and the Body of Christ to carry them out. After that, just before His ascension:

And Jesus came up and spoke to them, saying, "All authority has been given to Me in heaven and on earth. Go therefore and make disciples of all the nations, baptizing them in the name of the Father and the Son and the Holy Spirit, teaching them to observe all that I commanded you; and lo, I am with you always, even to the end of the age." (Mt 28:18)

"Even to the end of the age." Which age? The Church age? Or perhaps the age of the Kingdom Dispensation when the Jews are following the Sermon on the Mount? This age supposedly comes 2000 years after the resurrection. Why did Jesus bother to tell Peter, James, and John about this? Why did the Holy Spirit reproduce this life in the early Church and anywhere else that would listen to Him? If, as some have taught, the Sermon on the Mount is not for the Church age, then why did Jesus tell His disciples to **"make disciples of all the nations"**? Maybe the Great Physician was telling them to take His word to those that were sick. What did He tell them to teach the nations? **"Teaching them to observe all things that I have commanded you."**

Reading the Great Commission very literally, they were to go into this age and teach specifically those things. They were not to go about teaching whatever came along, but to propagate the actualization of the things Jesus had commanded. They were to bring those of every nation into the flow of the Spirit, the life, and the word from which salvation – as opposed to "die and go to heaven"- flow. We can be Gnostics and speculate some secret teachings that no one knows about, or we can be good 21st -century Protestants and teach abstractions derived from eschatological speculation and cloak it in the name "Age of Grace", or we can be believers and acknowledge Jesus' emphasis on the things He had openly spoken.

Maybe the twisted emphasis is why we see the church making converts but not disciples - the church no longer believes discipleship is for this age. And maybe that is why the Holy Spirit is relegated to the sidelines - or else to some cheap show run by a very wealthy miracle worker.

Yes, the Law was done away with, but not for the releasing of chaos, but for establishing the Law of Love.

Love does no wrong to a neighbor; therefore love is the fulfillment of the law. (Rom 13:10)

For the whole Law is fulfilled in one word, in the statement, "YOU SHALL LOVE YOUR NEIGHBOR AS YOURSELF." (Ga 5:14)

Bear one another's burdens, and thereby fulfill the law of Christ. (Ga 6:2)

If, however, you are fulfilling the royal law according to the Scripture, "YOU SHALL LOVE YOUR NEIGHBOR AS YOURSELF," you are doing well. (Ja 2:8)

The words of Jesus are the true understanding of that love, and, as we saw in talking about the Holy Spirit, the Holy Spirit comes when we keep the royal law- the law of love, which fulfills all other laws.

"In everything, therefore, treat people the same way you want them to treat you, for this is the Law and the Prophets." (Mt 7:12)

Now some would say, "You believe that Jesus got rid of the Law and now we're under the Sermon on the Mount". No, I believe just the opposite: we're not under it, it's under us- or better yet, it's within us.

When God moves by the Golden Rule (Mt 5:44&45), it is not because He is under that commandment, it is because

167

that commandment is inside Him - it is the expression of His heart. That commandment is not an obligation for Him, it is freedom; it is expression. By way of example: the rules of counterpoint are a great and limiting bondage for most music theory students: they were a way of unlimited expression for J. S. Bach. Sonnet form slows most people's written output to nil; it was a platform for some of Shakespeare's greatest work. The commandments of Jesus, as with everything else of truth, are foolishness to the Greeks, a stumbling block to the Jews. To us who are being saved, they release Christ, the power of God and the wisdom of God.

If Jesus' words come to us as carnal commandments, it is because **"that which is born of the flesh is flesh, and that which is born of the Spirit is spirit."** The carnal mind grasps neither the kingdom of heaven nor its ways; it can only treat them with the same mind with which we handle traffic laws and income taxes. If that is where we are then we had better hurry up and start keeping the Sabbath, obeying the dietary laws, and hoping that there is an altar in Jerusalem before we die so that a lamb can be slain for the atonement of our sins.

God almighty gave the Law through a mediator. God was not under that Law, He had no transgressions of His own to forgive, He was most Holy, He provided a Lamb, He built a temple, He sanctified a high priest, He did the work of a kinsman redeemer, He provided a city of refuge, He left the gleanings in the field so we might not starve. . . He who was not under the law demonstrated that the Law could be under Him. The Son of Man is Lord of the Sabbath - therefore He can do good on the Sabbath. Man was not made for the Sabbath, it was made for man; these things of God are made for us, by God, and the same Spirit that gave them to us is the administrator of them, just as the Spirit gave us the scriptures and is the final administrator of them.

Because the religious mind is working in the dark when it deals with divine truth, it can only put God's laws into human categories. Because something like the Sermon on the Mount is so contrary to human experience, something must be done. To the old man it is a more onerous burden than the Law of Moses: it will damn us all if it is the basis for our judgment, and that is the only way the religious mind can deal with it. The old man is subject to tree of the knowledge of good and evil; everything is a "do I have to" or "don't I have to." It will never be free because it will either be under Law, or under lawlessness.

One of the problems of our age is that we have dispensationalized away the truth. What that means is that every element of the life we're to live - whether we're talking about the Holy Spirit (oh, that was for the early Church) or the teachings of Christ (they were for Israel, so we don't have to do anything with them) or the Church (it will be coming down out of heaven at the end of the Millennium), is shipped into another time frame and the Church is left with very little to do on earth. We ultimately wind up living in an airy form of grace that leaves the world, which desperately needs the answers that a living Church can reveal, being given a watered down version of the truth, and no living example. The world is supposed to hate the Church because the Church upholds the ways of Christ. As it is the world hates the church for being a noisy special interest group that not only wants its own way all the time, but expects everybody to see the glories of Christ in all this.

Actually much of what Jesus taught is being lived out in the third world every day. Saints in Africa and parts of Asia and

South America are risking their lives every day to simply hold on to the name of Jesus. The underground Church in China has grown immensely during persecution. We will examine this briefly in a later chapter, but needless to say, it puts the churches in the affluent West to shame and exposes their doctrines for the empty vapor that they are.

Much of this happened because of the great struggle in the nineteenth century. Art and literature escaped into the past or the imagined future or the mythical far-away places. Philosophy mythologized history and de-mythologized the Bible; the conflicts with the final collapse of the Age of Reason and the coming of the new Industrial Age were enormous. The Church got backed into a corner and clung to Biblical inerrancy instead of the Bible; the fact of Jesus' deity instead of the living reality of His Lordship; the promise of heaven over there instead of the Kingdom that Jesus brought to this earth; the hope of heaven after we die rather than the life eternal that begins with the knowledge of Jesus; God in heaven instead of in our hearts; Jesus coming someday rather than the abiding presence of the Father, Son and the Holy Spirit. We came to believe in tomorrow because we were afraid of today. We started to believe in the future because we had thrown away the present.

It would be hard to overestimate how deeply the futuristic Romantic mind set has filled the Church and tainted her theology. She is left with nothing to do other than make converts who have nothing to do than make converts. Heaven is the fire escape and we receive the message of salvation out of self-preservation. This individualistic mind set has us catering to the 20th-century propensity for individualism which leaves the Church without the most effective witness- the testimony of changed lives bonding together by the power of the Holy Spirit, living daily by the Truth.

The question still arises as to the people who actually heard Jesus' words: were those words for His hearers or for us? Were those for the Jews in 1st-century Palestine, or the Jews in the Tribulation, or for the Jews at some other point in time for a "Kingdom Gospel"? After all, Jesus was preaching to the Jews, wasn't He?

Well, as a matter of fact, Jesus said He was not preaching to Jews. In fact He made it quite clear that He was preaching to me, and I most certainly am not a Jew.

While Jesus was travailing in the Garden of Gethsemane He poured out His heart to the Father. This is recorded in the Bible so that all might see the heart of the Father. He several times mentions the words that He gave His disciples. Notice how He refers to them.

"But now I come to You; and these things I speak in the world so that they may have My joy made full in themselves. I have given them Your word; and the world has hated them, because they are not of the world, even as I am not of the world". (John 17:13&14)

Here Jesus makes it plain: He is not speaking to His disciples as Jews, He is speaking to them as believers. In fact he says it again

"They are not of the world, even as I am not of the world." (Jn 17:16)

We read again in an earlier chapter

"If you were of the world, the world would love its own; but because you are not of the world, but I chose you out of the world, because of this the world hates you." (John 15:19)

171

In a stretch of divine faith He is referring to them as fully redeemed believers, even before His death and resurrection. Even before that dispensation, Jesus could view Peter and James and John as new creatures at that time because He was operating in eternity. His eyes could transcend time and He could see them as the born again. He could see them according to their calling, not according to their lineage. That is why in His teaching ministry He taught them openly, while only giving parables to the masses. Many in the masses were, in fact, Jews and nothing more. They never would be more. The words Jesus was teaching were to believers and to them alone. They were words that only a new kind of man could do anything with. The old kind of man could only make these words into law, or else say that they didn't matter because of a theological technicality.

The church in the West is withering because much that matters to God has been relegated to the scrap heap because of faulty theology. Jesus was never limited because of time. His sacrifice was eternal. Only the specific outpouring was located in time, and even that could be affected by faith.

An Account

She was desperate; her little daughter was vexed, cruelly vexed, by a spirit and no one could help. The situation was worsening, and the daughter was making life impossible for others, and was frequently endangering herself. The mother had exhausted all possibilities and there was nothing more to be done.

One day she heard that the Jewish miracle worker had come into the area. She had heard months earlier about this amazing person, what incredible power he had. But who could go to Galilee? Her little daughter could hardly even go to the neighbor's house much less take a trip like that, and she had no money to sustain them for the journey. God had brought that man to this village!

God had brought that very man to this very village - of course!!

God Almighty had brought the man she had been wanting to see to her village!!!

She found out where he was staying.

Now she was crying - wailing actually - a genuine disturbance, this gentile woman with her peculiar way of speech, her desperation. The Master didn't seem to be taking notice of her - why not just send her away? He had come to this area to be with his disciples and to teach. Now this.

She was pleading with Him.

But He answered and said, "I was sent only to the lost sheep of the house of Israel." (Mt 15:24)

Obviously not good enough. The wailing went on. Didn't she realize what dispensation this was? This was not the gospel of grace. This was not the ministry to the Gentiles, this was not the age when the Spirit of God was moving all over the world: this was part of the Age of the Law, and the emphasis was clearly on the Jews; merely a preparation for that time when the Gentiles would receive the offer of salvation. That was down the line - she would have to wait. Several steps were clearly missing and her lack of theological understanding was clearly to blame for the situation that was now unfolding.

And He was saying to her, "Let the children be satisfied first, for it is not good to take the children's bread and throw it to the dogs." (Mark 7:27)

173

Well, He had told her. Now leave us alone. The Master had agreed; this was not to be.

But out from the tortured soul of a woman in pain, but who had most certainly found her place in the scheme of things, came this assertion:

But she said, "Yes, Lord; but even the dogs feed on the crumbs which fall from their masters' table." (Mt 15:27)

To her it was simple: God had brought this man to this village for her daughter. That was certain. She had known that if only He would come. . .

And now he was here.

Then Jesus said to her, "O woman, your faith is great; it shall be done for you as you wish." And her daughter was healed at once. (Mt 15:28)

Faith had trumped dispensation. Some people live governed by time line theology, other people live by the eternal laws of the Kingdom of Heaven.

By faith Abel offered to God a better sacrifice than Cain, through which he obtained the testimony that he was righteous, God testifying about his gifts, and through faith, though he is dead, he still speaks. (Heb 11:4)

I'm not sure which dispensation Abel was part of, but since he was living by faith, his sacrifice was not limited to the times he lived in. Yes, he did not receive the promise, because that was to come, but he received the testimony that he died in faith - and he pleased God. Many people think that sacrifice and faith can't be mixed, but again- faith trumps dispensation.

All the heroes of *Hebrews* 11 were jumping ahead of what the times dictated, and as we live in faith, as we keep on seeing those things that are eternal, we too will be living with a view to an administration suitable to the fullness of the times, that is, the summing up of all things in Christ, things in the heavens and things on the earth. In Him (Eph 1:10)

Many talk as if there will be Jews and Gentiles and all the other distinctions in the future final kingdom. But if, as Paul asserts, that partition was torn down by Christ, how much more in eternity, when Christ is all in all? The breaking down of divine history for analytical purposes is handy enough, but when we then declare divine activity to be limited according to the time frames we have developed, we assume God to be very narrow in thought and action, and very much like us. To talk about the Age of Grace is a nice fence to put around a particular chunk of history, but don't expect to keep God in. God is active when He wants to be, where He wants to be.

The Dispensation of Grace did not begin its operation with Pentecost or the empty tomb, it began when "by faith Abel", or even earlier when God put a mark on Cain so people wouldn't kill him, or even earlier when God provided skins for the Man and the Woman - an operation of grace, though not through faith. God was busy before there were dispensationalists to tell Him what He could or could not do.

To be fair, there is truth to dispensational analysis, but we may not use it to say that the Sermon on the Mount is for later, and that somehow Paul's Gospel of Grace oversteps it. Paul's Gospel effectively puts the Sermon on the Mount as the life that the new man lives under grace. For the redeemed man this is the way of life the Spirit of God administers. In all Paul's exhortations the teachings of Jesus are front and center: center in life, center in ministry, center in the Church, and even center in evangelism. This was the way of life of the Church that swallowed up the Roman Empire, and many of the churches that did it were started by Paul.

12

ESCHATOLOGY AND THE WORDS OF JESUS

ESCHATOLOGY IS THE GREAT TRASH dump of theology. It is littered with the wreckage of dates for the second coming, a few hundred candidates for antichrist, timelines, charts, theories on the millennium; and on and on it goes. There is an ever changing stream of perspectives - winds of doctrine Paul calls them - concerning the Second Coming and the events that surround it. This is all rather fun when it is not taken seriously (one of those mind games that intellectuals are so taken with); the tragedy is the effect that it has on lives now. We live in the shadow of eternity, and our view of things future greatly affects the way we view the present. Even more so, it greatly affects our reasons for living, our goals, and our aspirations - or lack of them.

So often, rather than govern our lives by those things that God has told us for today, we allow ourselves to be run by an interpretation of the future. How many people have given up looking for work because "Jesus will be coming soon, anyway"? Not many, but some. How many people are not seeking His kingdom because there is nothing to seek once we are saved? Multitudes. And anyway - the kingdom isn't until the millennium, right? How many Christians have succumbed to lethargy because there is no reason for zeal? If there is no life of God to be had here other than the American Dream, why not "eat, sleep, drink and be merry, for tomorrow we fly"? No preacher would confess to these ideas, but none of them say much when the spiritual life of their flock is undermined by them. These things are open for anyone to see - and the world sees them.

With the spate of recent disasters (signs of the times) both man-made and natural, how much more pressing it is that we build our lives upon those things that are eternal, those things that God has revealed to us with all certainty. We are, in fact, to be as servants waiting for their master to return. We are to be as subjects waiting for their king to return, or as virgins waiting for the bridegroom to come and usher them into a banquet. These are clear simple pictures that the theologians have to work hard to cloud over. We have been given orders as to how to live and what to do. There is no theology that can contravene these orders.

Although it would be tempting, we cannot avoid the subject of Biblical prophecy since that subject is integrally intertwined with both doctrine and practice all through the New Testament. It also vitally affects every part of our lives. It permeates the moral teachings of Jesus and the apostle Paul. There are many passages which start out referring to ordinary things of daily life which wind up with references to the Lord's coming or the final judgment.

"He who receives a prophet in the name of a prophet shall receive a prophet's reward; and he who receives a righteous man in the name of a righteous man shall receive a righteous man's reward. And whoever in the name of a disciple gives to one of these little ones even a cup of cold water to drink, truly I say to you, he shall not lose his reward." (Mt 10:41&42)

Slaves, be obedient to those who are your masters according to the flesh, with fear and trembling, in the sincerity of your heart, as to Christ; not by way of eye- service, as men-pleasers, but as slaves of Christ, doing the will of God from the heart. With good will render service, as to the Lord, and not to men, knowing that whatever good thing each one does, this he will receive back from the Lord, whether slave or free.

And masters, do the same things to them, and give up threatening, knowing that both their Master and yours is in heaven, and there is no partiality with Him. (Eph 6:5-9)

And this I pray, that your love may abound still more and more in real knowledge and all discernment, so that you may approve the things that are excellent, in order to be sincere and blameless until the day of Christ; having been filled with the fruit of righteousness which comes through Jesus Christ, to the glory and praise of God. (Php 1:9&10)

According to the common theology, which so many preach, the way we live our lives is not important: after all we're saved, aren't we? Don't we all have a mansion just over the hilltop? Doesn't Pauline grace teach that nothing we do matters; that all of life for those who are believers in Christ is just marking time till we get carried off to heaven? We have a whole generation of Christians who really have no reason to live, and their young people know it and it is driving them away. Through Dispensationalism we have seen all of the Church

Age reduced to a parenthesis, a gap between the first coming of Christ and His second coming, during which the Church was to just go around getting people saved and wait for Jesus to come and take them away. While the theologians made very little of the effect of the parenthesis, the parenthesis did its work: we introduced the search for significance into the midst of the only people on earth who had a basis for significance-the Church. These popular theologies have left our young people very vulnerable to the diseases of this age: materialism, and the aimless despair that lies like a canopy over this whole culture. Unfortunately the shadow of eschatology hovers over the lives of most Christians far more than the shadow of the cross.

Because of the many views and the near impossibility of adequately dealing with them, rather than speculate on the future - when this or that will happen - we will occupy ourselves with the immediate question: in the light of the immanent coming of our Lord, how are we to act? What did the Lord give us to do to "occupy" till He comes? There are several parables on this subject as well as several other statements.

"Be on guard, so that your hearts will not be weighted down with dissipation and drunkenness and the worries of life, and that day will not come on you suddenly like a trap; for it will come upon all those who dwell on the face of all the earth. But keep on the alert at all times, praying that you may have strength to escape all these things that are about to take place, and to stand before the Son of Man." (Luke 21:34-36)

Without exaggerating, most popular theologies are not consistently comfortable with these verses which refer to the day of the Lord's coming. These scriptures tell us that we are to be sure that we are ready for the Day of the Lord. Now, according to the understanding that most people seem to have, the only thing to being ready is to have accepted Jesus Christ as Lord and Savior. Therefore, for the believer, there is nothing more, and God will be pleased with us in the last day. In any case, these verses are consistent with all the other teachings of Jesus; in several of His parables He stated that He would leave, and the disciples were to be ready for Him when He came back. Readiness would consist of having believed in Him and served Him, and having kept themselves unspotted from the world.

In Matt 25, we have three parables that deal with the return of Jesus Christ. They summarize what Jesus tells His disciples (not the Jews) about what they were to be doing in preparation for His coming.

The first is the parable of the ten virgins. (Mt 25:1-13) Five were ready and five were not. All had the expectation of going into the banquet. They were waiting for the Bridegroom. Five that were without oil in their lamps were unable to enter. They were not prepared.

The second is the parable of the talents. (Mt 25:14-30) As with the parable of the virgins, we have a waiting period. The servants have been given a task to do and the means with which to do it. It is important to note that these were servants entrusted with something: talents, i.e. money, and the master expected them to function with those talents. How would they have been able to handle a substantial amount of money? Well, they had been the master's servants and undoubtedly they had gone on errands with the master. Most probably they had been around the neighborhood helping their master with his trading, dealing with the master's goods under his oversight while he was with them. They would have had every opportunity to learn His ways, to learn whom to bargain hard with and with whom to be lenient. They would have known the master's view of these business contacts, and would have been prepared so as not to be hoodwinked by anybody. They would have known the value of the master's goods, and how he would have negotiated. They would have had insight into the mind of the master because he had taught them; therefore he would have expected them to do as he would do; he would have expected their business instincts to be trained and ready for work. He would expect that in his absence they would be able to carry on the business in the same way he would have. And that is the point of the parable.

The third is the parable of the sheep and the goats (25:31-46). This parable tells us how the nations will be judged. Those whom the Lord saw living by His precepts were ushered into life. Those who didn't think it mattered were ushered into punishment.

"Then He will also say to those on His left, 'Depart from Me, accursed ones, into the eternal fire which has been prepared for the devil and his angels; for I was hungry, and you gave Me nothing to eat; I was thirsty, and you gave Me nothing to drink; I was a stranger, and you did not invite Me in; naked, and you did not clothe Me; sick, and in prison, and you did not visit Me.' Then they themselves also will answer, 'Lord, when did we see You hungry, or thirsty, or a stranger, or naked, or sick, or in prison, and did not take care of You?' Then He will answer them, 'Truly I say to you, to the extent that you did not do it to one of the least of these, you did not do it to Me.' These will go away into eternal punishment, but the righteous into eternal life." (Mat 25:41-46)

"Lord, when saw we. . . .and did not. . ." They had no idea of how the Lord regarded His people. He regards them as inseparable from Himself. What we do with His people is what we have done with Him. This will be the subject of a later chapter.

Having referred to the teachings of Jesus on this, we come to the question we have all been waiting for: does Paul teach that we are waiting for a Lord who is coming back, and when He returns is expecting us to have fulfilled certain mandates? Will He be expecting us to have lived a certain way? To have treated His people a certain way? To have taken the things He has given and used them with wisdom and discretion? Are there people who have named the name of Jesus who have something to worry about upon the Lord's return?

But you, why do you judge your brother? Or you again, why do you regard your brother with contempt? For we will all stand before the judgment seat of God. For it is written, "AS I LIVE, SAYS THE LORD, EVERY KNEE SHALL BOW TO ME, AND EVERY TONGUE SHALL GIVE PRAISE TO GOD." So then each one of us will give an account of himself to God. (Romans 14:10-12)

Every knee surely meaneth me. Actually, if we have truly passed out of death into life, we will not enter into judgment because we will have allowed the Spirit of God to judge us. We will have entered into a new birth that is a continual renewing by the Holy Spirit. We will have walked in light that exposes all darkness. We will have washed our robes and made them white, having bowed our knees to Him in our daily lives. Judgment will have begun at the house of the Lord and we will already have completed the process.

Therefore whoever eats the bread or drinks the cup of the Lord in an unworthy manner, shall be guilty of the body and the blood of the Lord. But a man must examine himself, and in so doing he is to eat of the bread and drink of the cup. For he who

eats and drinks, eats and drinks judgment to himself if he does not judge the body rightly. For this reason many among you are weak and sick, and a number sleep. But if we judged ourselves rightly, we would not be judged. But when we are judged, we are disciplined by the Lord so that we will not be condemned along with the world. (1Cor 11:27-32)

There it is: judging ourselves. Paul uses the phrase when writing of Christians: disciplined by the Lord. Hebrews says that

"FOR THOSE WHOM THE LORD LOVES HE DISCIPLINES, AND HE SCOURGES EVERY SON WHOM HE RECEIVES." (Heb 12:6)

We who have experienced new birth are cleansed so that the Spirit of God may enter in and transform our lives and our hearts. We are disciplined as sons. Just as Jesus walked this earth as a Son under the chastening hand of the Father, so we walk this earth under the loving hand of Almighty God, with the Holy Spirit within us to lead and to guide, and to give us a spanking if need be. When the day is done, there is a reckoning, so that those who have served will receive their due reward. Our goal is that we not be condemned along with the world.

For no man can lay a foundation other than the one which is laid, which is Jesus Christ. Now if any man builds on the foundation with gold, silver, precious stones, wood, hay, straw, each man's work will become evident; for the day will show it because it is to be revealed with fire, and the fire itself will test the quality of each man's work. If any man's work which he has built on it remains, he will receive a reward. If any man's work is burned up, he will suffer loss; but he himself will be saved, yet so as through fire. (1Cor 3:11-15)

Jesus Christ is the foundation that is laid. There is none other. The work we do in this life may be of eternal value or it may not. The day will show it all for what it is worth. Many will have nothing to show; many will have much to show. Those whose works are burned will suffer loss. This particular salvation comes at a cost. People who want to be saved need to know that there are several options in the scriptures for salvation; Paul speaks of salvation past, present and future. The life we live now has something to do with salvation. There are levels of what will go with us- thirty-fold, sixty-fold, one hundred-fold. Also, those people who are always looking forward to the day of the Lord might take note that there could be less after that day, rather than more. And that is Paul's opinion.

For we must all appear before the judgment seat of Christ, so that each one may be recompensed for his deeds in the body, according to what he has done, whether good or bad.

Therefore, knowing the fear of the Lord, we persuade men, but we are made manifest to God; and I hope that we are made manifest also in your consciences. (2Cor 5:10-11)

Paul says "we." We must all stand. Not just they, but we. He, Paul, wants to be manifest in their consciences so that the message will get through.

For momentary, light affliction is producing for us an eternal weight of glory far beyond all comparison, (2Cor 4:17)

Notice it does not say that "Grace" is working an eternal weight of glory. (Actually it is grace that is at work even in this, but most people don't understand Paul's use of grace.) It does not say that saying the sinner's prayer is working a weight of glory. Actually many preachers won't say that anything is working an eternal weight of glory; they don't see that there is anything to be worked. Paul did. Our lives in Christ have eternal consequences.

185

For this you know with certainty, that no immoral or impure person or covetous man, who is an idolater, has an inheritance in the kingdom of Christ and God.

Let no one deceive you with empty words, for because of these things the wrath of God comes upon the sons of disobedience. Therefore do not be partakers with them; (Eph 5:5-7)

Paul is telling Christians that immoral and impure people can't hide behind Jesus. Jesus offers us clean hearts, clean minds, clean robes and a clean place to dwell. He expects us to take Him up on all His offers. The Christian life is a life of purification, the continual exchange of rags for riches. There is no hiding in the light; we abide in Jesus so that the pollutions of this age have no place in us.

Instruct them to do good, to be rich in good works, to be generous and ready to share, storing up for themselves the treasure of a good foundation for the future, so that they may take hold of that which is life indeed. (1Tim 6:18&19)

Something about the future is stored up by this life; something about good works. They don't save us, but they are what we were created for. Lots of people have "received Jesus" and have not received His life in any sense of the word. It lies dormant within them, partly because they have not been instructed in the ways of life.

Slaves, in all things obey those who are your masters on earth, not with external service, as those who merely please men, but with sincerity of heart, fearing the Lord. Whatever you do, do your work heartily, as for the Lord rather than for men, knowing that from the Lord you will receive the reward of the inheritance. It is the Lord Christ whom you serve. For he who does wrong will receive the consequences of the wrong which he has done, and that without partiality. (Col 3:22-25)

Everyone will receive for the wrong they have done. Therefore even Christian slaves are to watch how they act toward godless masters. If there is no consequence for the believing slave, then the whole exhortation falls flat. These slaves are to be like the slaves Jesus talked about who are watching and waiting, knowing there is a Master who will return, and that there are rewards.

Do this, knowing the time, that it is already the hour for you to awaken from sleep; for now salvation is nearer to us than when we believed. The night is almost gone, and the day is near. Therefore let us lay aside the deeds of darkness and put on the armor of light. Let us behave properly as in the day, not in carousing and drunkenness, not in sexual promiscuity and sensuality, not in strife and jealousy. (Ro 13:11-13)

Watch our P's and Q's. Why? The master is coming. In any case, Jesus could have said that. Actually, He probably did: Paul was probably just reminded by the Spirit of what Jesus had taught.

so then let us not sleep as others do, but let us be alert and sober. (1Th 5:6)

"But keep on the alert at all times, praying that you may have strength to escape all these things that are about to take place, and to stand before the Son of Man." (Lu 21:36)

Jesus calls us to attention, just as Paul does.

Be on the alert, stand firm in the faith, act like men, be strong. (1Co 16:13)

More than that, I count all things to be loss in view of the surpassing value of knowing Christ Jesus my Lord, for whom I have suffered the loss of all things, and count them but rubbish so that I may gain Christ,

and may be found in Him, not having a righteousness of my own derived from the Law, but that which is through faith in

Christ, the righteousness which comes from God on the basis of faith, that I may know Him and the power of His resurrection and the fellowship of His sufferings, being conformed to His death; in order that I may attain to the resurrection from the dead. Not that I have already obtained it or have already become perfect, but I press on so that I may lay hold of that for which also I was laid hold of by Christ Jesus. (Php 3:8-12)

Paul obviously thought this was optional. Paul was obviously so convinced that there was nothing to be done and nothing to be gained in the area of sanctification that he was just out passing out tracts to get people saved. After all - doesn't Paul say that Jesus laid hold of us so that after we go to heaven we can have Jesus's life?

These ideas are preposterous to the point of being ludicrous, but they are what an increasing number of preachers are asking us to believe.

But when we look closely at this passage we see Paul giving flesh and blood expression to Jesus' admonition,

Then Jesus said to His disciples, "If anyone wishes to come after Me, he must deny himself, and take up his cross and follow Me. For whoever wishes to save his life will lose it; but whoever loses his life for My sake will find it." (Mt 16:24&25)

Paul knew that God laid hold of us for a purpose, and that after salvation we were to lay hold of the principles of life so that not even death could hold us back. We were to lay hold of the life that Jesus bought for us, the life that is described in the Lord's teachings, the life that the Holy Spirit completes in us as He leads us into all truth and reminds us of all the things that Jesus taught us. He didn't want to be found with just righteousness that was imputed because of a prayer, but the righteousness that is imputed because of a walk by faith, just like that of

Abraham, and Enoch, and all the other heroes of faith. Their walk wasn't "works" in the negative sense because it was God who was at work within them. It was grace just as Paul says

But by the grace of God I am what I am, and His grace toward me did not prove vain; but I labored even more than all of them, yet not I, but the grace of God with me. (1Cor 15:10)

It was no longer Paul that lived, but Christ that was living in him. Faith and grace and labor were inseparable in him by the work of the Holy Spirit, and that is what the Holy Spirit was sent to do.

Now may the God of peace Himself sanctify you entirely; and may your spirit and soul and body be preserved complete, without blame at the coming of our Lord Jesus Christ. Faithful is He who calls you, and He also will bring it to pass. (1Thes5:23&24)

The multi-dimensional working of the Spirit of God, encompassing the totality of the person is why the Spirit was given - that all parts: body, soul, and spirit, might be preserved.

And this I pray, that your love may abound still more and more in real knowledge and all discernment, so that you may approve the things that are excellent, in order to be sincere and blameless until the day of Christ; (Php 1:9&10)

He is not talking about a one shot deal of imputed righteousness or the whole thing becomes meaningless. Jesus is not a one shot deal: He is the air we breathe, the words that we speak, the life that we live. Grace is imparted to us daily as we walk with Jesus - that is why Paul's letters speak so often of grace and peace. Our walk with the Lord is grace working through righteousness to produce believers that are poor in spirit, who do unto others as they would have others do unto them, who turn the other cheek, and everything else that Jesus taught. Paul is talking about a seed of truth that is planted in the heart

189

of every believer. We are to guard that seed, nurture that seed, and allow the Spirit of God to bring forth that life in us so that we are blameless in the day of Christ, as Jesus and Paul taught.

But put on the Lord Jesus Christ, and make no provision for the flesh in regard to its lusts. (Ro 13:14)

It should strike people as odd that Paul would teach that we should put on the Lord Jesus Christ, yet having done so, turn around and say that what came out of Jesus's mouth was not pertinent to us. In fact, Paul's plain teaching was that the life we have been given is to come to a certain point of maturity by the day of Christ. Gifts have been given, just as they were to the servants in the parable, and when the master comes back, it's interesting that the apostle of grace is most antsy that all would be in order on that day.

I thank my God always concerning you for the grace of God which was given you in Christ Jesus, that in everything you were enriched in Him, in all speech and all knowledge, even as the testimony concerning Christ was confirmed in you, so that you are not lacking in any gift, awaiting eagerly the revelation of our Lord Jesus Christ, who will also confirm you to the end, blameless in the day of our Lord Jesus Christ. (1Cor 1:4-8)

Paul, in his own thinking, was never far from the coming of the Lord. It is obvious in the way he viewed himself

For I am conscious of nothing against myself, yet I am not by this acquitted; but the one who examines me is the Lord. Therefore do not go on passing judgment before the time, but wait until the Lord comes who will both bring to light the things hidden in the darkness and disclose the motives of men's hearts; and then each man's praise will come to him from God. (1Cor 4:4&5)

It was difficult to spend so much time on this subject because it is hard to isolate all these scriptures on this subject without sounding judgmental, but Paul was very focused on bringing the churches he had founded to a certain level of growth by the time the Lord came. This goal permeates his writings, and demonstrates the effect Jesus' teachings about the last days had upon him in reference to almost every sphere of life.

13

CAESAR AND THE WORDS OF JESUS

THEY CAME AND SAID TO Him, "Teacher, we know that You are truthful and defer to no one; for You are not partial to any, but teach the way of God in truth. Is it lawful to pay a poll-tax to Caesar, or not? Shall we pay or shall we not pay?" But He, knowing their hypocrisy, said to them, "Why are you testing Me? Bring Me a denarius to look at." They brought one. And He said to them, "Whose likeness and inscription is this?" And they said to Him, "Caesar's." And Jesus said to them, "Render to Caesar the things that are Caesar's, and to God the things that are God's." And they were amazed at Him. (Mk 12:14-17)

IT IS A familiar story: another attempt to trick Jesus. The answer is equally familiar: "**Render to Caesar the things that are Caesar's, and to God the things that are God's.**"

This is a very clever answer that got Jesus off the hook in a tight situation. Most people marvel at the wisdom of it and how well it shut down the harassment. But is it just a clever answer that Jesus gave in a particular situation to escape a trap? Maybe. Or perhaps it is in the Bible to show us the kind of wisdom that is in Jesus Christ to deliver believers from the schemes of wily men, which it certainly does. But let's take that statement at face value, separate from the circumstances in which it was said, and examine it to see if there is anything in it that will shed some light on the believer's relation to Caesar, by which we mean worldly government and, by extension, the society in which we live.

This is another classic "is it?" or "is it not?" question that was put to Jesus. The Pharisees would give Jesus two choices and make Him choose one or the other of them. After all-there are only two possibilities and only one could be correct. Right?? My money is mine and God wants me to do the right thing with it, so what am I supposed to do with it? Caesar or God? The answer is obviously a no-brainer, except that Jesus declares the question to be a no-brainer. Jesus again by-passes their categories; neither alternative describes the realities of the Kingdom of God. Jesus is not limited to their either/or.

After they asked Him, Jesus had them look at a coin. Now, there were two kinds of currency back then: Roman currency, with Caesar's image, and the temple currency with no image at all. This unique currency was a special concession by the Roman government to prevent a Jewish meltdown; the temple could not have coins in it which proclaimed the lordship of Caesar. Since the Jews were out to keep their temple clean (well. . . sort of. . .), they obviously could not use the Roman coins, so a truce agreement emerged: Roman coins were not legal for the temple, and temple coins were not legal for the outside world. This dual currency situation provided the necessity for the money changers that were there in the temple. Pilgrims from foreign lands needed temple currency so they could give lawfully unto the Lord. How could they give money stamped with Caesar's image to God Almighty?

In His response, all Jesus did was to ask the Pharisee to show Him a coin. Whose image? Caesar's? Well, God won't have it. Very clever, an absolutely water tight response.

But it is more than a clever answer: it is a clear statement of a principle of the Kingdom of God that governs our relationship with this world. We cannot take Caesar's coin into the temple. To the degree we tote his image around we cut ourselves off from the holy things of God. The early Church maintained an identity very separate from that of the society around it, but was nevertheless able to have an effective witness in that hostile culture. The teachings of Jesus were living truth to them, and so they were able to function in God's Kingdom right here on earth. That is one of those graces that the preachers will tell us was for that age, which was, in fact, the beginning of this age.

Earthly freedom is not without its limits, and Jesus makes it clear that many of those earthly limits restrict the free working of the Kingdom of God. We not only cannot serve God and Mammon, Jesus tells us specifically that Mammon cannot serve us: it is a master, not a subject. Every person who has tried to have Mammon serve him has run into this hard reality, and most did not even know it. Jesus also tried to convince us that Mammon cannot serve God. That truth has been lost on every church in North America.

The Kingdom of God does not readily share space with the kingdom of the world; God's kingdom breathes purer air and operates on different principles. Now, that does not mean that God is not at home on this earth: in the Incarnation, God indeed dwelt among us in flesh and blood in the person of Jesus Christ. Through the redemption effected by the death, burial and resurrection of Jesus Christ, the very Spirit of God dwells in man, here and now in those who are redeemed: those who have taken Jesus to be their Lord by faith.

For He rescued us from the domain of darkness, and transferred us to the kingdom of His beloved Son, in whom we have redemption, the forgiveness of sins. (Col 1:13&14)

In this passage Paul sees the whole transaction as a change of government, a transfer to God's kingdom. Governments do not allow people to split their allegiance when under their jurisdiction: as a U.S. citizen I cannot expect to be under U.S. law when I visit France. I certainly cannot drive on the right side of the road when I visit England, though that might have to do with more than just traffic laws. I certainly don't expect the same right to express my views if I visit Cuba. I don't care if people visit this country and have strange opinions and unusual customs, but I deny their right to hijack the governmental process and make me pray five times a day toward Mecca. Governments are exclusive domains, and when they overlap, as do federal and state governments or federal and provincial governments, there are tomes of laws and armies of lawyers to define where one ends and the other begins. The dividing line between my right to govern myself and the federal government's right to govern me has kept an entire legal system hopping for two centuries.

The domain carved out by the Redemption has become the stage on which the Kingdom of God plays out its role. The Kingdom moves by divine laws and is governed by God and whomever He delegates. The world's stage is under contract to a different management and we can't be part of both. These governments don't mix. We read in scripture

Jesus answered and said to him, "Truly, truly, I say to you, unless one is born again he cannot see the kingdom of God." Nicodemus said to Him, "How can a man be born when he is old? He cannot enter a second time into his mother's womb and be born, can he?" Jesus answered, "Truly, truly, I say to you, unless one is born of water and the Spirit he cannot enter into the kingdom of God. That which is born of the flesh is flesh, and that which is born of the Spirit is spirit. Do not be amazed that I said to you, 'You must be born again.' The wind blows where it wishes and you hear the sound of it, but do not know where it comes from and where it is going; so is everyone who is born of the Spirit." (Jn 3:3-8)

There are two realms, flesh and spirit, and we cannot even see the spirit realm without a special operation of God. When Jesus said, "That which is born of the flesh is flesh," He was stating a principle of divine government: things hark back to the authority that created them. Not only is the offspring of like DNA with the parent, it is also subject to the same laws and under the same authority. We, in our old Adamic nature, are merely flesh and can serve nothing but flesh. We cannot please God (Rom8:8). The spirit man is not under the government that the man of the flesh is under: he who is born of the Spirit is like the wind, which the flesh cannot grasp.

OK - so what? Where does all of this leave us in regard to earthly governments, as well as how we function on planet Earth? If all that we start out with is earthly then shouldn't we just give it all to God?

But here's the rub: how do I give it all to God? Only one kind of currency circulates in God's kingdom. My talents in their original state are as useless to God's kingdom as my spiritual gifts are useless in a bank. I suppose I might use them to some purpose with someone standing in line, but it is extraneous to any financial transaction going on in the bank. Any spiritual gift or ministry that I may have will not improve my interest rate or help in the cashing of checks. Jesus said that what was Caesar's was to be rendered to him. If it bears his image, then give it to him. The human organizations don't fit through the narrow gate. The endless programs and promotions to build up churches: if they bear Caesar's image, i.e. if they are not of divine origin, then they can only bring forth flesh. We cannot offer them to God because He cannot use them, and they cannot serve Him.

The big houses in suburbia are dead weight in the race. The expensive life styles are the testimony to the lordship of Mammon. The fact that Christians got hammered so hard in the economic chaos is testimony that God didn't give us all that stuff and God isn't going to do much to help us keep it. He who had no place to lay His head is not out for the preservation of someone's 400–square-foot master bedroom - especially when so many of His saints have no place to lay their heads. We see indigenous ministers and pastors all over the world in need of bicycles or motorcycles or donkeys to help them get from place to place for the spread of God's word, while preachers in this country have cars, boats, RVs and airline mileage from the church credit card to take them nowhere in particular.

On the other hand, we are so quick to drag the holy things out into a public spectacle. The Christian TV networks and organizations with their star today, scandal tomorrow preachers have made the Christians a laughing stock. They are a mockery for the heathen and a shame for the sincere. Then we drag out our high moral standards and our indifference to the poor. What sense is the world going to make out of that?

Render to God the things that are God's. How quick to give on Sunday morning a widow's mite of the thing God cares least about – money - and how stingy to give what God cares most about: hearts turned over to Him. This is no place to talk about the cultivation and the nurturing of the Anointing - that portion of the Spirit of God that He has given to each believer for the common good - but that Anointing, offered up to God and yielded for His service means far more to the Kingdom than the glitzy, cheap religious displays that haunt the dial when people are looking for something to watch. Jesus went into the wilderness and couldn't keep the crowds away. We bring the church into the living room and watch it decline, both in numbers and in content.

Shallow spirituality for a superficial age: we plant icons and bumper stickers in front of the world and then put on a sorrowful face when they don't come to Jesus. The world doesn't see a Church that has offered to God the things that are God's, and at the same time they see a church that has too many things of Caesar's and that is as slow as the heathen to render them unto Caesar.

When Jesus heard this, He said to him, "One thing you still lack; sell all that you possess and distribute it to the poor, and you shall have treasure in heaven; and come, follow Me." (Lu 18:22)

Here is Jesus telling us to get rid of the baggage in our lives. We are to throw off the ballast so that we can be more efficient in our service. But even more than that, things that pertain to this earthly here and now life, things that have Caesar's image if you will, have a claim on us. Our money belongs to us and the tax man. Our house belongs to us and the city tax man. All the things we have are part of a system, part of a network of relationships that are highly intertwined and severely limiting. All our freedoms operate within a defined set of restrictions. My property is mine but my dog can make only so much noise even if he is on my property. The tree is on my land but the branches hang over onto your property and it is my responsibility if my tree branch takes out your roof. I may live in a free country, but I am not free to drag race police officers on the public roads. The old saying that my freedom ends where your nose begins is very true - and governments are more and more nosey.

We live in a free country, and we have practically worshipped that freedom, regarding it as our sacred liberty. Yet our sacred liberty to worship is another person's sacred right to an abortion, and another person's right to same-sex marriage with full spousal rights, and another person's right to use Wall Street to pillage investors, and another man's right to get a clever lawyer and use the court system to financially plunder his wife and then make her pay alimony to support him. . . And the list goes on forever. We have bought in to a series of lies, and freedom is one of them. Just like the world after decades of unimaginable prosperity: the poor are hungry and the government is bankrupt; the church, after two hundred years of unrivaled freedom sees herself locked out of the life of God, marginalized in society, and we scratch our heads and wonder why. Or we try to use the machinery of "freedom," which generated this mess in the first place, to restore things to the way they used to be.

Render to Caesar. . . What would that have said to the disciples of Jesus? They had very little that Caesar had claim to: little money, little property. That commandment would not have hit them hard because they were keeping the rest of the words of Jesus. The Sermon on the Mount liberated them from Caesar in a very real way. He still had authority to terminate the functioning of their bodies on earth, but He had no dominion over the operations of their inner man. His decisions might cramp their style, but not the functioning of the Spirit.

He who has nothing of Caesar's will not have much to render to him. Jesus's goal was to keep us untrammeled from the world's claims, its thought patterns, its values, etc. The more I have that belongs to God, the more claim He has on me. What things I have of Caesar's bind me to Caesar. We think those things are neutral but they are not.

The Apostle Paul tells us:

I know and am convinced in the Lord Jesus that nothing is unclean in itself; but to him who thinks anything to be unclean, to him it is unclean. (Rom 14:14)

That has been taken by many people as a statement to liberate us to free participation in everything around us. If nothing is innately unclean **in itself**, then obviously I can enjoy everything: pork is clean to me, clothing of cotton/polyester blends are clean to me, that beautiful women over there is clean to me. . .

Well, actually she is not. Not everything is clean to me because that ring on her finger says that she is not "in herself:" she is in a relationship. This ring on my finger says that I am not merely "in myself:" I am in a relationship whereby there are boundaries. The nature of marriage is such that woe to the one who tests the boundaries. As with marriage, so with many other things: my freedom to partake is actually limited, but it is not limited by ceremonial uncleanness. In dealing with the Jewish law Paul makes statements about Christian liberty that have nothing to do with the untrammeled "liberty" that so many Christians shout about. Not all women are mine, even as not all pharmaceuticals are mine, nor are they clean to me.

Paul tells us that **"nothing is unclean in itself."** The thing most of us fail to recognize in dealing with this whole issue is that there are many, many things that are not just "in themselves." Sure - cocaine is not unclean in itself, but by nature it hollows-out a special place for itself in the lives of its fans. Cocaine does not like to be "in itself." The only place where cocaine is not unclean in itself is in the sterile environment of the laboratory, or possibly in certain prescription applications. To the alcoholic a bottle of whisky is not ever strictly "in itself;" it operates relationally, as do a host of other things we come in contact with.

All things are lawful for me, but not all things are profitable. All things are lawful for me, but I will not be mastered by anything. (1Cor 6:12)

All things are lawful, but not all things are profitable. All things are lawful, but not all things edify. (1 Cor 10:23)

When heroin enters the world Paul's question must be asked, "Does it edify?" In many other things as well the question must be asked, "But does it edify?"

Fornication is unclean in itself precisely because it defines a relationship wherein a man ceases to be "in himself" and comes into relationship with a woman with whom he is not to have that kind of relationship. He ceases to be "in himself." He and the woman have become one flesh.

Or do you not know that the one who joins himself to a prostitute is one body with her? For He says, "THE TWO SHALL BECOME ONE FLESH." (1Co 6:16)

When Jesus declared all foods clean He did not authorize the rich man to eat everything on the table. He did not transfer gluttony from the list of vices to the list of virtues; He merely set foods free from the Old Testament ceremonial law and placed them back in the dominion of the Father. Though we are to see foods separate from the Mosaic dietary law, we are not to see them in isolation from the law of love: nothing dwells in that isolation. They were not even liberated from the commandments **"Thou shalt not covet"**(AV) and **"Thou shalt not steal."**(AV) They still function in their sphere of operation- too much food will kill, just as too much money will twist the soul. He thus declared all foods clean, but none are clean to the glutton; his cravings take steak and chocolate and place them in a shrine.

God created gold, but man created money. The second that gold became money - and there is a difference - it became something unique. Man took that element from God's domain. He gave it a definition and a place alien to God. The books on economics will tell you that the development of money was a revolutionary breakthrough in the realm of trade and commerce. It was, but it did not spring out of man's desire for smooth commercial transactions: man set gold aside at an earlier time than that. This was an operation of the heart, not just a manifestation of an innate business instinct. Man ripped gold off the periodic table and ensconced it in his pantheon far above hydrogen and sodium: he gave it a place in his heart. He separated gold from the mineral world of carbon and boron and set up his own special value system and oriented his life to it in an inordinate way. **"Nothing is unclean in itself"** ceased to apply to gold because gold was now a part of the heart of man; man could only see it with his heart, not with his eyes.

This helps illustrate the real issue in our relations with Caesar and the world: our relationship with God is a covenant relationship. We have been espoused to one Husband, and

He is jealous. Mammon is another suitor. The systems of this world: the education system, the financial system, the communications system, the religious system, as well as the governmental system, the medical system, all are under the domain of another king and are their agents. God tells us to render unto Caesar that which is Caesar's because God can't use it, and He tells us to render unto God the things that are God's- the world does not want them anyhow.

Speaking of money. . .

14

THE WORDS OF JESUS AND THE MINISTRY

"FOR WHO IS GREATER, THE one who reclines at the table or the one who serves? Is it not the one who reclines at the table? But I am among you as the one who serves. (Lu 22:27)

"just as the Son of Man did not come to be served, but to serve, and to give His life a ransom for many." (Mt 20:28)

Then He poured water into the basin, and began to wash the disciples' feet and to wipe them with the towel with which He was girded. (Jn 13:5)

"If I then, the Lord and the Teacher, washed your feet, you also ought to wash one another's feet. For I gave you an example that you also should do as I did to you. Truly, truly, I say to you, a slave is not greater than his master, nor is one who is sent greater than the one who sent him. If you know these things, you are blessed if you do them. (Jn 13:14-17)

For you know the grace of our Lord Jesus Christ, that though He was rich, yet for your sake He became poor, so that you through His poverty might become rich. (2Co 8:9)

Wealth, power, security, approval. . . .

As this is written, the world is in the middle of a severe economic crisis. Nations have been devastated, millions have lost vast sums that they saved, and unemployment has reached record levels. This current economic distress gives many simple lessons in how the modern world functions, or, shall we say, how it dys-functions. Article after article has been written to show how all these complex wheelings and dealing have operated. It has all been very fascinating to see how people in charge of giant companies have sent those companies to the bottom because they had only a short-term personal interest in their company. Their bonus only depended on the quarterly or yearly growth of the company, not on market share, development of new products, or long-term viability within the industry. They were literally betting the company on this year's profit statements.

One of the primary lessons to be garnered from all this has to do with conflicts of interest. In many companies the chief executives, officers, and managers were not, in fact, representatives of the company; they were employees whose long-term interests in the company were not synonymous with those of the company. While piloting the ship, they saw an iceberg with gold on it. The logical thing to do was to ram the ship into the iceberg, grab the gold, and row off in a lifeboat while the ship sank. Too bad about all those investors whose pension funds were tied up in that company and who needed a viable company to invest in. The fact of the matter is that those investors were the company; the managers and directors who thought they were the company most definitely were not. Give them a salary that depends on today's profits and sure enough, there would be profits today - from the sale of the scrap metal from the company.

When I go to a car dealership to buy a car I meet a salesman. Now that person is commissioned to sell a car and I am out to buy a car. That is neat: the salesman can sell me a car at near cost, and I am happy, the salesman is happy, but the car dealer goes broke. No one is representing the interests of the car dealership. That is why the third person comes in: the sales manager. I am not overly fond of sales- managers, mainly because I have never seen one. This invisible third person really has the power to make everyone nervous because he is the deal maker or the deal breaker. He is out to keep the dealership in business. All parties need to be represented for there to be a sustainable business, and the sales manager is the final necessary representative.

The salesman has a classic conflict of interest: he does not represent the dealership, even though he works for the dealership. He is just selling a car. In reality he could be giving me too good of a deal. He has minimal long-term interest in the dealership, but only that it should stay in business. The overall health of the dealership is not his concern. For me it does not matter if the dealership stays in business or not - I can always find someone who will sell me a car. As for the car manufacturer, it is no problem of theirs whether the dealer stays in business or not; they just want cars sold- and lots of them.

Now let's look at the current church situation; it is one giant conflict of interest. If I go to a typical church on Sunday morning, they have a building. They have some programs: probably a Sunday school for all ages, some youth meetings, various services and activities. They probably also have steady financial obligations, whether it's the light bill or the building fund or the latest campaign to repave the parking lot. As a going business entity they have their own needs which have to be met regardless of Jesus.

Well, the chief salesman of this church is the pastor. It is his job to sell me on his church's version of the Kingdom of God. Now this product comes in more shapes and sizes than cars - in fact each church has its own. If I go to two Ford dealerships I expect the Fords to be the same in each one. I do understand that the service departments may be a bit different, but even then the product is the same. As far as servicing goes I can always have a different dealership - or the local garage - service the car. But in the church, I get a different product wherever I go. It is like going to a hamburger joint and finding out that their hamburgers have neither meat nor buns, but that this really is the best hamburger - "it's all in the relish" you know.

The pastor's job is to maintain the local church- the dealership in our analogy. Ultimately he has no over-riding interest in the Kingdom of God. There are churches that have done famously without even believing there is a Kingdom of God.

Now, my previous paragraph needs a little modification because all churches - well most churches anyhow - believe they are selling you Jesus first and then an additional options package. They tell you the old, old story and get you to Jesus (He's the free give away) and then try to sell you a lot of very costly add-ons, similar to a service contract, but with some important differences which most people who are new to Jesus will accept. In practice this does little to change the previous paragraph because although Jesus may (or may not) be presented the same at all dealerships, most are not going to tell you much about what you have acquired. They will not tell you how to get your new Lamborghini out of first gear. They will tell you that the wonderful new life you have will really not kick in till you die, that the wonderful feeling you have cannot be relied on, and that most of the great features of the wonderful new product that you have acquired won't be available till in fact, you are dead. Your new Lamborghini really will go faster than 50 miles an hour, but the transmission is locked and, anyway, you really won't be able to do much with it right now but keep up with traffic. But in order to get a bit more use out of your new car you will need to visit their service department every Sunday morning, and get your kids there so they can get their sports car of the future today.

Yes, they sell you Jesus, or rather a retainer, and ostensibly Jesus is the same at all dealerships and only the options differ, and they really are important. And every once in a while at church you will hear the story of someone who got his car into high gear and the wonderful power that was there.

This pastor is like the salesman and the sales manager all rolled into one. If he says that this is what the kingdom of God sells, well then, this is what this dealership will sell. Long on activities, short on worship? No problem, this is how we do it. Loads of community service and a formal ritual on Sunday? This is how we do it. I can buy it or not, but this is what I will get at this dealership. The Kingdom of God itself has no direct say; God may or may not get anything from all of this. The local entity, often called a church, goes on whether it has any authorization from God or not. It has an independent life. The minister has a pure conflict of interest if ever there was one.

The whole business is even stranger when we factor in how much of Jesus is available without the local church and its pastor. Even the local pastor will tell me I can get Jesus without him or the local church. Most will tell me I have direct access. They will tell me that church is not necessary, but yet it is necessary, or at least massively helpful. . . Well, the local church really is a support system for my recent acquisition of Jesus, and if I want to get full use of Him, I will need their services. I will need other people who have acquired Jesus and learned what benefits He can provide here. Or so they say.

Now, it is not as if there was no guidebook for Jesus. God's purpose is well laid out in the guidebook and it is easy to find out most of what I need to know about Jesus. If I look in the guidebook of the Kingdom of God, I read certain things. These things are more uniform from front to back of the guidebook than the salesmen like to admit. There is a lot about God in there, and there is a lot about how we are to conduct our lives. We learn, for example, about righteousness, self- control and the judgment to come. Great Pauline themes these, Jesus' sayings are full of them, and the Old Testament as well. Some churches put differing emphases on them, many evangelical churches saying we have little or nothing to do with righteousness - it's all done for us. Self- control? Ditto. And then we have nothing to do with the last judgment because we get a pass on that one too. Actually, Jesus does talk about those who have passed from death to life not entering into the judgment, but then preachers tell us that we can't experience that life until after we die - and it all gets very confusing. And in any case, the people don't look like they have passed from death to life. But they preach long sermons on it. And the guidebook says it is true. . . .

The local church's role? Self- perpetuation. The religious establishment's role? Self- perpetuation. The pastor's role?

Build a local church, get converts, etc. It all boils down to self- preservation.

We see all the preachers on the platforms on the TV religious broadcasts. They are the gospel marketers. It is their job to interpret the Christian faith to the masses. They get paid by commission, just like any salesman: the more the results, the bigger the church; the more bodies in the seats, the more the pay. They go to salesman school to learn how to sell Jesus; what works and what doesn't. Then they go out and preach about Jesus - or something. Maybe they preach about heaven someday – (not much in the guidebook about that: most of the passages talk about being on earth, except that we are seated with Him -right now- in heavenly places).

Like the salesman but unlike the sales manager, they sell to the lowest bidder, except that the Kingdom of God is not what grows: the churches grow. Long term benefits to the Kingdom? Irrelevant. What does God have to say about all of this? No one is asking. These are the only sales agents God has, and He either stands behind this and watches the Kingdom go to ruin, or He walks away and no one misses Him.

Not much here to attract the hungry.

So what about the ministry?

"Whatever house you enter, first say, 'Peace be to this house.' If a man of peace is there, your peace will rest on him; but if not, it will return to you. Stay in that house, eating and drinking what they give you; for the laborer is worthy of his wages. Do not keep moving from house to house. Whatever city you enter and they receive you, eat what is set before you; and heal those in it who are sick, and say to them, 'The kingdom of God has come near to you.' But whatever city you enter and they do not receive you, go out into its streets and say, 'Even the dust of your city which clings to our feet we wipe off in protest against you; yet be sure of this, that the kingdom of God has come near.' "I say to you, it will be more tolerable in that day for Sodom than for that city." (Mt 10:5-12)

Nothing. Not even a mailing list.

If you read the New Testament, Jesus sent twelve men into the world with a very contrary message, with no hope of gain in this world. All their treasures were in the next life. All were hidden in God, and any attempt to mix this life with the next life meant forfeiture of the divine favor. They had no stake in anything other than the Kingdom of God, and their prosperity depended on maintaining the purity of God's message and the faithfulness of their service. Only thus would they maintain God's blessing. As we have reiterated and will continue to reiterate, this pattern is being reproduced in a few places, primarily in under-developed poverty areas where missionaries, both indigenous and gringo, have given their lives to the spreading of the truth of Jesus Christ. This method still does work, and it still preserves more of the purity of the gospel message, because if people are risking death for a message then they jolly well want it to be God's message, not just the smiley faced stuff before the fund raising.

The system that Jesus set up is closer to the heart of the Old Testament practice than we like to admit. In the Torah you had one tribe set aside for God. It was without an inheritance. They were scattered all throughout Israel and it was their job to teach in the area where they lived and to go up to Jerusalem to help with the temple worship. They had no inheritance - at least as a tribe. God was their inheritance.

Then the LORD said to Aaron, "You shall have no inheritance in their land nor own any portion among them; I am your

portion and your inheritance among the sons of Israel. To the sons of Levi, behold, I have given all the tithe in Israel for an inheritance, in return for their service which they perform, the service of the tent of meeting. The sons of Israel shall not come near the tent of meeting again, or they will bear sin and die. Only the Levites shall perform the service of the tent of meeting, and they shall bear their iniquity; it shall be a perpetual statute throughout your generations, and among the sons of Israel they shall have no inheritance. For the tithe of the sons of Israel, which they offer as an offering to the LORD, I have given to the Levites for an inheritance; therefore I have said concerning them, 'They shall have no inheritance among the sons of Israel.'" (Nu 18:20-24)

The idea was that they were to be dedicated to the Lord, having nothing but the tithes as their support. The only church to be maintained was the temple - which got them into trouble because, with an established priesthood, they in fact had a program to maintain. In their villages, though, the Levites would prosper only as the Lord's service prospered. They had no buildings (synagogues were a later addition) so they were merely scattered about to help raise the spiritual level of the people. As people gave tithes and offerings out of their love for the Lord then the tribe of Levi would prosper. If the people's love grew cold then that tribe would not thrive.

Getting back to today, as long as the ministry is saddled with an inherent conflict of interest, then the church system will continue to chew up and spit out even some of the most able, zealous and anointed of God's servants. As long as the life of a church is tied up so deeply with self-maintenance, then what position will the Kingdom of God have in the scheme of things? People with the calling of God to be in ministry, whatever that is, have an obligation to stay separated to the word and prayer; whole true churches have an obligation to keep the ministry free to dedicate themselves to the word and prayer.

Will the people of God support a servant of God? I don't know. I suspect that they will- and even if they don't, I suspect that God will. At least that is what He said.

But in any case, all these teachings were given to a living Church. They were given to a Church where the word of God was upheld, the believers were contrary to society in the most effective way: in lives lived in direct opposition to the values, norms and assumptions of the status quo. The biggest threat to a minister was torture - not merely the possibility that he would have to take his seminary degree somewhere else and find another church.

When Jesus came to earth, He came as the representative of the Father. He represented the long term interests of the Father and of the Father's kingdom.

Therefore Jesus answered and was saying to them, "Truly, truly, I say to you, the Son can do nothing of Himself, unless it is something He sees the Father doing; for whatever the Father does, these things the Son also does in like manner. For the Father loves the Son, and shows Him all things that He Himself is doing; and the Father will show Him greater works than these, so that you will marvel." (Jn 5:19&20)

So Jesus said, "When you lift up the Son of Man, then you will know that I am He, and I do nothing on My own initiative, but I speak these things as the Father taught Me. And He who sent Me is with Me; He has not left Me alone, for I always do the things that are pleasing to Him." (Jn 8:28&29)

"I speak the things which I have seen with My Father; therefore you also do the things which you heard from your father." (Jn 8:38)

Jesus had no conflict of interest; He was not on a commission, He was the Heir. If He messed up the Kingdom, then He would inherit a messed-up kingdom. He was an accurate representative of the Father, the Father's interests were upheld, and the Father's name was set forth clearly. Everything about the Kingdom was in the able hands of Jesus Christ.

The typical pastor, on the other hand, has a classic conflict of interest: his salary is not dependent on the long-term prosperity of the Kingdom. The overall good of the company is not his to know. Look at the account of the rich young ruler

As He was setting out on a journey, a man ran up to Him and knelt before Him, and asked Him, "Good Teacher, what shall I do to inherit eternal life?" And Jesus said to him, "Why do you call Me good? No one is good except God alone. You know the commandments, 'DO NOT MURDER, DO NOT COMMIT ADULTERY, DO NOT STEAL, DO NOT BEAR FALSE WITNESS, Do not defraud, HONOR YOUR FATHER AND MOTHER.'" And he said to Him, "Teacher, I have kept all these things from my youth up." Looking at him, Jesus felt a love for him and said to him, "One thing you lack: go and sell all you possess and give to the poor, and you will have treasure in heaven; and come, follow Me." But at these words he was saddened, and he went away grieving, for he was one who owned much property. And Jesus, looking around, said to His disciples, "How hard it will be for those who are wealthy to enter the kingdom of God!" The disciples were amazed at His words. But Jesus answered again and said to them, "Children, how hard it is to enter the kingdom of God! It is easier for a camel to go through the eye of a needle than for a rich man to enter the kingdom of God." (Mk 10:17-25)

There are few pastors who would have enough of the Spirit of God to tell a rich man that he must unload if he really wants to be a disciple. Most could not put the spiritual well-being of the man above the economic needs of the church. Most would say how fortunate the church was to have a rich man in the congregation. Most would not challenge an affluent congregation to down- size their houses, their cars, their lifestyles. Most pastors have not down-sized their own. If they get an offer from a bigger church they look at the offer, agonize over it for a week, and then accept it as God's blessing on them. How many churches lure ministers by a bigger salary? They get what they paid for: a bigger salaried hireling. The higher purposes of God limp on.

How many pastors of today would even know who the itinerant preacher - this Jesus fellow - was? He could come into their churches (and undoubtedly He has come into some) and have to sit where the usher put him. The songs and the sermon would go on as per usual. No one would have known who the Visitor was who came into the church that morning. Only those who walked with Jesus can truly minister Christ, or know Him.

Lest we think that is only the way things go in the high formal churches, He could walk into some of our freewheeling churches and the only difference is that He could seat Himself, then would have to endure a high decibel rock concert, before sitting silently as the local preacher exhorted one and all on how to apply the word to their lives. In a home church He would find His words countered by others and possibly receive encouragement not to have doctrinal certainties.

In any case the churches roll on. What about "**Sell all that you possess and give**"? We might use it for a Sunday sermon text on the subject of giving and do a song and dance around what it would have meant for the early church. Those words of Jesus have no place in our churches because they have no place in our religious culture, nor have they a place in our hearts. We are too sophisticated. So we hire ministers whose values are a subset of the culture of our day - minus abortion, gay rights, and the far left - and produce more of the same.

Where is the minister who will stick to the small church with little salary? Where is the church builder who goes from place to place - little place to little place - and brings forth living examples of the Body of Christ, and then moves on? We don't even hold up Jesus' words as an abstract ideal. Where is the minister who shuts up on occasion and lets one have a song, one have a prophecy and one have a teaching?

When we consider the words of Jesus as they relate to the ministry we must first look at what the ministry is supposed to minister. Let's look again at the Great Commission.

And Jesus came up and spoke to them, saying, "All authority has been given to Me in heaven and on earth. "Go therefore and make disciples of all the nations, baptizing them in the name of the Father and the Son and the Holy Spirit, teaching them to observe all that I commanded you; and lo, I am with you always, even to the end of the age." (Mt 28:18-20)

If we are to disciple the nations in the things that Jesus taught us, maybe it requires ministry with something other than a seminary degree. Maybe an educated understanding of the religious world is a liability rather than an asset. Maybe people who have become as little children or newborn babes and been taught by God from scratch should have a voice. Maybe saints need to be ministering to God's people, not just the professionals. Maybe people who have been schooled by God in the Sermon on the Mount, in the teachings and the –gasp!- commandments of Jesus should have a voice in our churches. (Look again at 1Cor 14:37; 1 Thess 4:2; 2 Thess3:6; 2 Thess 3:12 for those who think Paul was allergic to commandments.)

Where can we go now for examples of ministry? Maybe the Church in Africa can help us out in showing us the qualities necessary for growth of the true Church. Maybe the Church in China can show us a bit about leadership. Maybe the prayer lives of the saints in Korea would be something to consider as exemplary for ministerial candidates. How tragic it would be for the Church in North America to have won so much of the world and lost the true message of Jesus Christ. How tragic the number of eager young people who want to serve God and are thrown into the religious system: it devours the faithful and lives off their dedication. Like the harlot of Revelation 17, it drinks the blood of the saints, sustaining its life by draining theirs, and then uses its energy to commit fornication with the kings of the earth. As true a picture of modern evangelicalism as it is a picture of the medieval Catholic church.

Never have the teachings of our Lord Jesus Christ spoken so directly to the needs of the Church, and society, and never have the churches been so deaf to their message. Again, the commission says to make disciples of the nations. How can non-disciples do that?

15

THE WORDS OF JESUS AND THE BODY OF CHRIST

AND HE FELL TO THE ground and heard a voice saying to him, "Saul, Saul, why are you persecuting Me?" (Acts 9:4)

The classic understanding is that Saul first met Jesus on the Damascus road. This is typical of our refusal to take Jesus at His word. What Jesus actually said can be reduced to, "Saul, we have met before. What is your issue with me?"

Saul met Jesus when Stephen was being stoned. Saul thought they were stoning an apostate Jew; Jesus said they were stoning Him. When Saul broke up that meeting in the lower quarter it was Jesus that he threw in jail. When the believers in the small towns around Jerusalem were arrested by Saul, it was Jesus who was arraigned. Saul was now going to Damascus to throw Jesus in jail- at least that is how Jesus saw it. Why shouldn't we take His word for it?

"The one who listens to you listens to Me, and the one who rejects you rejects Me; and he who rejects Me rejects the One who sent Me." (Lu 10:16)

We were instructed not to take it personally when persecution would come: the persecutors really hate Jesus. In the gospels Jesus laid the doctrinal foundations for an understanding of the Body of Christ, making it clear that His indwelling of His people was more than just a figure of speech. The Body of Christ was being explained in these scriptures already quoted when Jesus said:

"The King will answer and say to them, 'Truly I say to you, to the extent that you did it to one of these brothers of Mine, even the least of them, you did it to Me.'" (Mt 25:40)

"Then He will answer them, 'Truly I say to you, to the extent that you did not do it to one of the least of these, you did not do it to Me.'" (Mt 25:45)

Jesus portrayed Himself as being inseparable from His people. The blessings poured out upon the least of them were poured out upon Him. The abuse heaped upon the least of them was heaped upon him. This is the Body of Christ. This is how the Lord of the entire universe indwells His Body. Paul would spend the rest of his life working out the implications of Jesus' greeting to him on the Damascus road.

But just as Jesus declared Himself inseparable from His people, so he also declared Himself inseparable from the Father. He came openly declaring the Father to mankind- or at least to those who would believe Him- and openly declaring His union with the Father. The Father was being declared on the mountain when Jesus spoke. Heaven was being revealed because Jesus was in vital union with the Father. He was not giving personal opinions. When He healed someone He was not just showing off the miraculous powers that He had. When He cast out demons He was not trying to impress His audience: He was revealing the Father. Jesus lived by the power of the Father. The Father was abiding in Him and He was abiding in the Father.

Hatred of Jesus was hatred of the Father.

"If I had not done among them the works which no one else did, they would not have sin; but now they have both seen and hated Me and My Father as well". (John 15:24)

Dishonor to the Son was dishonor to the Father

so that all will honor the Son even as they honor the Father. He who does not honor the Son does not honor the Father who sent Him. (John 5:23)

The Father and the Son were in each other.

Jesus said to him, "Have I been so long with you, and yet you have not come to know Me, Philip? He who has seen Me has seen the Father; how can you say, 'Show us the Father'? Do you not believe that I am in the Father, and the Father is in Me? The words that I say to you I do not speak on My own initiative, but the Father abiding in Me does His works. Believe Me that I am in the Father and the Father is in Me; otherwise believe because of the works themselves". (John 14:9-11)

Jesus ascended to the Father and then made provision that His people might have a living attachment to Him in the same way that He was attached to the Father.

"As the living Father sent Me, and I live because of the Father, so he who eats Me, he also will live because of Me." (John 6:57)

Even as the Father and the Son were in each other, so the believer and Christ are in each other.

221

"In that day you will know that I am in My Father, and you in Me, and I in you." (Joh 14:20)

Let's look at how Paul puts some of this.

He who descended is Himself also He who ascended far above all the heavens, so that He might fill all things. (Eph 4:10)

Filling all things- that must at least mean His followers, and it must mean the totality of our being. It is not speaking of fallen angels when it says, "fill all things;" it means us. It means our mouths, our minds, our emotions, our thoughts. It means our bodies pulsating with the life of Christ. It means that Jesus' servants are not living their own lives, but His life. Much quoted is

For to me, to live is Christ and to die is gain. (Php 1:21)

What that literally means is

For you are all sons of God through faith in Christ Jesus. For all of you who were baptized into Christ have clothed yourselves with Christ. There is neither Jew nor Greek, there is neither slave nor free man, there is neither male nor female; for you are all one in Christ Jesus. And if you belong to Christ, then you are Abraham's descendants, heirs according to promise. (Gal 3:26-29)

Here Paul is saying that in Christ the distinctions are wiped out: there are no Jews; God is not dealing with them as Jews. There are no men or women- God is dealing with them all as sons. There are no slaves and free- all are Christ's bondservants and slaves of no man. Now if God has done away with those things, how much more are we to be done with black and white, Americans and Chinese, high society and low? How much more putrid in God's sight is the elevation of the distinction between middle class and lower class, Baptist and Methodist, PhD. and dropout? How much more odious is our salute to the political right or the political left? The poor in spirit, i.e. those whom the world despises, are the blessed. Again we read

Do not lie to one another, since you laid aside the old self with its evil practices, and have put on the new self who is being renewed to a true knowledge according to the image of the One who created him—a renewal in which there is no distinction between Greek and Jew, circumcised and uncircumcised, barbarian, Scythian, slave and freeman, but Christ is all, and in all. (Col 3:9-11)

This is a realm in which Christ fills all things and is all things. Christ is life, and in Him we are new. We are now inseparable from Him. Reality is now Christ in His Body: once more the fullness of God manifest in this earth. Once more Jesus is walking this earth doing good and healing. Once more the good news is being preached. Every day Jesus is thrown in jail. Every day Jesus is reviled. Every day there are people who are blessed because they give Him a cup of cold water. Every day there are people who are blessed because they visit Him in jail. Every day people are blessed in that, as they have done it to one of the least of His brethren, so they have done it to Him. Certainly these are words for this dispensation - they can apply to nothing in the past, and they were written to the Church. Surely Jesus rejoices as His servants stand fast in the principles that He laid out. The one who is sent is totally in the place of the Sender. In the Bible this is not a diplomatic idea- a kind of legal fiction. Oh no, the very presence of Christ is in His body.

and said to them, "Whoever receives this child in My name receives Me, and whoever receives Me receives Him who sent Me; for the one who is least among all of you, this is the one who is great." (Lu 9:48)

"He who receives you receives Me, and he who receives Me receives Him who sent Me." (Mt 10:40)]

Jesus gave us access to the heart of God, and He also gave the heart of God access to us. Jesus died that the Spirit of God could dwell in us. In simple English, that means that He died that He might carry the heart of the Father into the depths of the creation- not so we could be saved and die and go to heaven, but that we might live on this earth right now, and prevail right here on this earth, right now, and take the very heartbeat of the Father with us everywhere we go right here on this earth, right now.

God poured Himself into the Son. Once more, in Jesus, there was an avenue for God to express His heart. When the Son of God reached out to touch a leper the power of the Father was there to heal. When Jesus opened His mouth to command the demons, the Father was using that opening to drive them out. When the Son of God, in obedience, opened His mouth to teach, then the Father had an opening to declare the heart of the Father. When the Son of God Was moved with compassion, God had a vehicle to express the fullness of His love.

When a believer opens His heart to another then the compassion of God has a means. When a believer moves in faith, then the Father has a portal to demonstrate the life that is within Him. When believers latch onto doctrines that say we are not "under" the Sermon on the Mount, or that the teachings that Jesus revealed from the mouth of the Father are for another dispensation, then most assuredly there is little opening for the Father to demonstrate His power. When we buy into the idea that we are merely saved to tell others, then the message will be limited to lifeless words and dead works. However, when we grasp the truth by faith that we are to be the living manifestation of Jesus Christ on this earth, then we will find God giving us the power of an endless life. Now, while it is true that <u>we</u>

may not go to hell because we don't "keep" the Sermon on the Mount, it's equally true that many of our children are hell-bent for destruction because that divine content was missing from our lives as parents. If we are just saved so we can 'die and go to heaven' then God does not have a vehicle for His purposes here on earth, and He really does not need our services in heaven. All the talk about heaven that Christians do – heaven is here in us and we are there in it. That's Paul's gospel:

I pray that the eyes of your heart may be enlightened, so that you will know what is the hope of His calling, what are the riches of the glory of His inheritance in the saints, and what is the surpassing greatness of His power toward us who believe. These are in accordance with the working of the strength of His might which He brought about in Christ, when He raised Him from the dead and seated Him at His right hand in the heavenly places, far above all rule and authority and power and dominion, and every name that is named, not only in this age but also in the one to come. (Eph 1:18-21). . . . and raised us up with Him, and seated us with Him in the heavenly places in Christ Jesus (Eph 2:6)

For you have died and your life is hidden with Christ in God. (Col 3:3)

that He would grant you, according to the riches of His glory, to be strengthened with power through His Spirit in the inner man, so that Christ may dwell in your hearts through faith; and that you, being rooted and grounded in love, may be able to comprehend with all the saints what is the breadth and length and height and depth, and to know the love of Christ which surpasses knowledge, that you may be filled up to all the fullness of God. (Eph 3:16-19)

That is also the perfect picture of Christ in us and us in Him, which is also what Jesus prayed that His death might accomplish-

"I do not ask on behalf of these alone, but for those also who believe in Me through their word; that they may all be one; even as You, Father, are in Me and I in You, that they also may be in Us, so that the world may believe that You sent Me. The glory which You have given Me I have given to them, that they may be one, just as We are one; I in them and You in Me, that they may be perfected in unity, so that the world may know that You sent Me, and loved them, even as You have loved Me." (Jn 17:20-23)

That is Jesus' classic statement of the Body of Christ. The implications of all of this were not lost on Paul: if we are in Christ and Christ is in His Body, then we are not only vitally attached to Jesus Christ, we are vitally attached to the Father and to everyone who is His. This is the understanding behind Paul's statements

I do not speak to condemn you, for I have said before that you are in our hearts to die together and to live together. (2Cor 7:3).

Either this is religious hyperbole or it is eternal truth. Either this is just some mealy-mouthed neo-orthodox newspeak, or this gives us a clear understanding of the heart of an apostle and an insight into just how far the apostle Paul carried his understanding of the Body of Christ. After all, if Christ indwells me and I am in Him, then I can be with Him anywhere He goes- even into the heart of my brother. Paul often tells us of his inextricable link with his brethren.

For I, on my part, though absent in body but present in spirit, have already judged him who has so committed this, as though I were present. In the name of our Lord Jesus, when you are assembled, and I with you in spirit, with the power of our Lord Jesus, I have decided to deliver such a one to Satan for the destruction of his flesh, so that his spirit may be saved in the day of the Lord Jesus. (1Cor 5:3-5)

These are incredible words. I guess I really should get a few commentaries out and see how Bible literalists treat this. (In any case I suspect that I take this far more literally than they do). The point is that Paul has communion with other believers, whether he's there or not. He has the care of all the churches- in a prison cell. This is the Body of Christ. The Body of Christ is where barriers are torn down so that believers become one. The Body of Christ is where it is fulfilled that

'You shall not take vengeance, nor bear any grudge against the sons of your people, but you shall love your neighbor as yourself; I am the LORD'. (Le 19:18)

We have already seen who our Neighbor is- He is the one who pours in the oil and the wine regardless of a person's color, nationality, political affiliation, economic status, or denomination. Those who abide in the realm where none of those barriers exist will love every believer as themselves because they are all wrapped up and tied together with each other. I used to wonder about that verse, wondering if that meant I had to love myself more in order to love others more. It was insoluble. Now I realize that my brother is part of me- that Paul really meant it when he said

For just as we have many members in one body and all the members do not have the same function, so we, who are many, are one body in Christ, and individually members one of another. (Ro 12:4&5)

Paul really meant it when he said

for now we really live, if you stand firm in the Lord. (1Th 3:8)

He really was loving his neighbor as himself. Paul was being consistent with the totality of scripture when he said

I have sent him back to you in person, that is, sending my very heart, (Phm 12)

If then you regard me a partner, accept him as you would me. (Phm 17)

The work of Christ had made Paul inseparable from all who belonged to the Lord, and he loved them even as himself. In Paul's heart there was no Greek or Jew, no circumcised or uncircumcised, barbarian, Scythian, slave, or free, black or white; there was only Christ. Jesus' prayer in John 17 had come to fulfillment in Paul, and Paul both demonstrated its fulfillment and labored to bring it about in the churches, fully in accordance with the teachings of our Lord. This Epistle to Philemon, written at the same time as the Epistles to the Ephesians and the Colossians, shows Paul's entire theology of the Body of Christ wrapped up in an ordinary human situation, and every bit of it in line with the teachings of our Lord.

The words of Jesus lead us into the Body of Christ, not as a doctrinal entity, a series of dogmas which we accept with a yawn, but His teachings lead us down the road to the flesh and blood reality of the Body of Christ, and all of a sudden "**Love Your neighbor as yourself**" becomes not merely a choice or a possibility, but it can become a reality. This happens when "**Blessed are the poor in spirit**" so dominates our hearts that we love those people who God loves. It is then that we see the reality of "**do not worry about tomorrow**" because we are seeing the hand of God moving in His Body today.

To reiterate: when Paul, on that memorable day on the Damascus road, ran into Jesus for the umpteenth time, he received an understanding from the Lord that would define his ministry: the revelation of Jesus Christ as Lord and the revelation of the Body of Christ. Jesus had said that there were things

He could not yet tell His disciples, and some of those things most certainly were given to Paul. Yes, Paul will carry them farther than the others, but the foundation was Jesus Christ, whose foundation was the Father.

Paul really did believe that God's will should be done on earth as it is in heaven, and that was the end to which he labored.

16

THE WORDS OF JESUS
AND THE PERSECUTED
CHURCH

I GET A MONTHLY NEWSLETTER from a missionary association that funnels money to indigenous missionaries. As I read it regularly I am struck with the lives and witness of many of the people in the brochure. The monthly prayer and needs list covers countries all over the world, from Cambodia to Brazil, from Jordan to the Sudan. The needs range from money to feed hungry children in an African village to bicycles to allow pastors in South America to cover more ground. There's an occasional church roof, need for five hundred Bibles in an obscure language, a PA system to allow young people to go into villages and put on music programs or show the Jesus Film. One also hears that pastor so and so in India got mugged and needs help with medical bills, or maybe just prayer, or that

saints in Cambodia are feeling real pressure- that means per-
secution- and need prayer support or money for the orphaned
children of a pastor. Or the churches in China got messed up
because of the recent earthquake and need money and prayers,
as well as blankets for others who lost everything.

Simple needs for simple people. I don't get the impres-
sion that they are accepting their lot with stoicism; it's more
like they realize that this is the cup that the Lord has put before them and so they do it with at least a measure of joy. It
sounds like someone forgot to tell them that **"Blessed are the
poor in spirit"** is no longer in force. They need to understand
that God is handing out blessings and that the gospel of grace
leaves us in line for prosperity and blessings, wealth and abundant life. They've missed it.

Of course, in the newsletter that comes one also reads
about the growth of the Church. Not just a few people saved,
but people- large numbers of people- coming out of heathen-
ism and starting new churches; whole villages coming out of
darkness; the Church in China stronger than they were when
they started. Nobody believes the government's figures for
how big the Chinese underground Church really is. People in
North Africa are breaking free from Islam because Bibles were
sent there, prayers went up, love was ministered, and lives were
changed.

I haven't noticed them wringing their hands about their
young people, what is to become of the Church, or "what
are things coming to?" Maybe in a few places that is going
on under the surface, but it sure does not seem like it. God's
Church is the place to be in Africa and Asia especially. The
gospel is being articulated by people who have been foolish
enough to believe that, **"Blessed are you when people insult**

you. . ." These are people who bless those who persecute them; people who share the little they have with the destitute people around them; people for whom the world holds no special appeal; who know it as the prison house that holds many who dearly long to be free.

I will be careful not to tell them that they have missed their dispensation. I will do my best to make sure that they don't worry about whether they will be "left behind" or not. I will try to make sure that the latest evangelism program that comes out does not make it to their shores. Hopefully they will not hear that we really don't have to go through the great persecution. We'd hate for them to lose the cup that they have drunk so nobly, and wind up with the lukewarm water that characterizes the churches of the West today.

CONCLUSION

THERE ON THE BEACH STOOD the elders of the church at Ephesus. Paul had sent for them with some urgency, so they knew the situation was important. He wanted to share a few moments with these beloved friends who had stood with him in trials and tests. They had seen him in the crucible of persecution, and some of them had suffered for adhering to the good news that Paul had brought. Now he was giving them their final charge. As he spoke they realized that they would probably never see Paul again.

So what instructions did Paul give to a church which would from henceforth be on its own? What important words of guidance did the apostle to the Gentiles give them?

He told them of how he had come and preached the gospel to them, how he was going to Jerusalem, not knowing what would transpire there, and then his final words to them,

"And now I commend you to God and to the word of His grace, which is able to build you up and to give you the inheritance

among all those who are sanctified. I have coveted no one's silver or gold or clothes. You yourselves know that these hands ministered to my own needs and to the men who were with me. In everything I showed you that by working hard in this manner you must help the weak and remember the words of the Lord Jesus, that He Himself said, 'It is more blessed to give than to receive.'" (Acts 20:32-35)

Luke would have us believe that the final word that Paul spoke to a Gentile church was that they should help the weak and remember Jesus' words concerning giving. That sentence that Paul quoted is the Sermon on the Mount in a nutshell. It is a statement of divine values that overturns tomes of current teaching. It turns us on a course that steers 180 degrees away from the "he who dies with the most toys wins" mindset of our day that harasses the weak for their lowly position. It tears at the heart of the "me" centered religion of our day that proclaims a man-centered universe more surely than Ptolemy ever did. They come fully against the rich liars who preach the prosperity gospels that leave millions of believers poorer in all ways than when they started out.

Notice also Paul's use of the word "grace." His is not the grace most people hear about in church. This is not the cheap pop-culture stuff that tells us that, "Love is not having to say 'I'm sorry'." This is the grace of a lover- the jealous Lover who will not have His Bride anything other than clean- clean before God, before the angels, and before all mankind. No demon will be able to say- "They love God because He let them get away with everything." None of the scoffers will be able to say, "Those Christians don't really love Him- they just love His benefits." Oh no- millions are paying a heavy price right now that all may know that they love God, and their testimony is making a tremendous impact on those countries. Grace is reigning in righteousness unto eternal life in many countries all over the world this very moment. This is the grace that cleanses. This is the grace that brings forth God's will, carried out on earth even as it is in heaven.

Your kingdom come. Your will be done, On earth as it is in heaven. (Mt 6:10)

This is the plain teaching of the whole Bible, from start to finish. Man fell, as described in Genesis 3, and the rest of the book is the story of God undertaking to restore this earth to union with God and His ways. The purpose of Calvary was not that we might inherit streets of gold to walk upon; it was that we might become a city of gold like pure glass (Rev 21:18) that He might walk in.

Or what agreement has the temple of God with idols? For we are the temple of the living God; just as God said, "I WILL DWELL IN THEM AND WALK AMONG THEM; AND I WILL BE THEIR GOD, AND THEY SHALL BE MY PEOPLE. Therefore, COME OUT FROM THEIR MIDST AND BE SEPARATE," says the Lord. "AND DO NOT TOUCH WHAT IS UNCLEAN; And I will welcome you. And I will be a father to you, And you shall be sons and daughters to Me," Says the Lord Almighty. (2Cor 6:16-18)

His purpose was that we might become a dwelling place of the Spirit of God that He might have a base of operations on this earth so that this earth might be shown the ways of God. So that in praying **"Our Father who is in heaven"** we are truly proclaiming a literal Father who disciplines, instructs, loves and guides sons, and not the father proclaimed by so many Protestants who is more distant than the god of the deists, and more of an icon than anything that liturgical religion proclaims. But oh yes. . . He wants to bless you and bless you. . .

So Jesus said to them again, "Peace be with you; as the Father has sent Me, I also send you." (Joh 20:21)

God did not send His Son to this world to tell the world about faraway places and streets of gold. He did not send His Son into this world to proclaim a superior ethic that we might emulate. He did not send His Son into this world so that Paul would be able to formulate doctrines for us to believe. God did not send His Son into this world so that we could build churches and watch our young people go to hell. God did not send His Son into this world so that we could have conferences on healing and watch people die, conferences on the Holy Spirit and watch people be powerless, conferences on family relations and watch divorce and domestic violence increase; God sent His only begotten Son so that we might be born of the Spirit.

"The wind blows where it wishes and you hear the sound of it, but do not know where it comes from and where it is going; so is everyone who is born of the Spirit." (Jn3:8)

Those who are born again are mysteries to the rest of mankind. They do not work by the same principles as the rest of mankind; they do not have the same values: they do not return evil for evil, they bless those who persecute them, when asked to carry the load a mile they carry the load a mile, and then an extra mile. Those who are born again do not think like the Republican (Conservative) Party or the Democratic (Liberal) Party for the simple reason that God Almighty cannot think like either of those alien entities. We have the Spirit of God Who searches out the deep things of God- not the latest buzz on when the Rapture will take place.

There is a vast world of spiritual experience available for those who are the Lord's, and most of the believers in the West have opted for the image of the Beast, not the likeness of the Son. Those who are born again are like the wind- they come from an unseen origin. They move by different laws because those who are born again have access to the heavenly places now.

even when we were dead in our transgressions, made us alive together with Christ (by grace you have been saved), and raised us up with Him, and seated us with Him in the heavenly places in Christ Jesus, (Eph1:5&6)

This is in fulfillment of Jesus' prayer

"Father, I desire that they also, whom You have given Me, be with Me where I am, so that they may see My glory which You have given Me, for You loved Me before the foundation of the world." (Jn17:24)

If all of this is true, what should we do about it?

Nothing.

Absolutely nothing.

There is no program, no formula, no list of items.

Having said that, the next thing is to point out that it says in Psalms

Your word I have treasured in my heart,

That I may not sin against You. (Ps 119:11)

The power of life is in spirit and in truth: they have their own dynamic; they know what to do. Blood-bought sons of the living God have the Spirit of God in them. That Spirit knows the heart of God, and when He gets inside us He knows what to do. We read,

And He was saying, "The kingdom of God is like a man who casts seed upon the soil; and he goes to bed at night and gets up by day, and the seed sprouts and grows — how, he himself does not know. The soil produces crops by itself; first the blade, then the head, then the mature grain in the head." (Mark 4:26)

In our next volume of this series we will talk about the seed. We will see the principles inherent in all forms of life. We will look at how life was meant to grow, and what was necessary to bring life forth. Only by moving according to the principles of life will we ever be able to experience anything of God's life in this earth.

In the meantime, is there anything we should do?

I could say that we need sorrow (Paul recommended that to the Corinthians 2Cor 7:9-11). Someone would make a rule out of it. I could tell you about sackcloth and ashes- Jesus said that Tyre and Sidon would have repented in sackcloth and ashes if they had seen the miracles that Jesus performed in Galilee. I can just see the article in one of the mainline Christian magazines- not to mention the local newspaper- after they made it public. But in any case, sackcloth is against the temper of the times. I could tell about putting to death our members which are on the earth (Col 3:5), however, since it is in the word, better to let the Spirit lead us into it.

Let's just eat the truth. Let its sweetness delight our tongues and let its power become bitter in our bellies. Let truth join with Spirit in the inner man and maybe an attic or two will be cleaned out of the accumulated extras. Maybe people will start to join together in spite of denominational lines. Maybe people will realize that they have space for someone else in that large suburban home. Maybe God's people will realize that the poor and the humble are blessed, and that it is in fact more blessed to be among the blessed than to be among the affluent. Maybe if people absorb the truth, speak the truth, live the truth, think the truth, just maybe some will find their minds renewed. Maybe some will enter into the kind of prayer that the heavenly hosts see fit to add their incense to. Maybe some will be given to hospitality. Maybe some will find the grace to start speaking the word of healing and not set up an earthly ministry to commercialize it. Maybe denominational lines will be broken down and the Body of Christ will be called together from the four winds of heaven. Maybe some stuck up whites will visit a black church and park themselves there every Sunday for a year and let God do something in their lives, instead of trudging around the same little religious treadmill they have for the last two decades.

Maybe.

Maybe some will get before God until hatred is out of their lives. Maybe some will pray until they forgive their parents for the abuse they suffered as children. Maybe some Christians will seek God's face long enough to recognize that their attitudes are just sheer prejudice, and then stay before God until those attitudes are gone.

Maybe.

But we must trust that "The zeal of the Lord of Hosts will perform it."

We've seen the Spirit of God move in many ways in the last 100 years. Everything that is begun gets buried under the denominational- sectarian spirit that rules the heart of man. The kingdoms of fear start to put up fences and protect their turf- and the little pet doctrine they've nurtured to distinguish themselves.

What is needed is dedication to the truth, and an emphatic renewal of the vision that faith, hope, and love are central to the outworking of the purposes of God in this dispensation, in the last dispensation, in the next dispensation, on earth even as it is in heaven, now and forever. Amen.

Now to Him who is able to establish you according to my gospel and the preaching of Jesus Christ, according to the revelation of the mystery which has been kept secret for long ages past, but now is manifested, and by the Scriptures of the prophets, according to the commandment of the eternal God, has been made known to all the nations, leading to obedience of faith; to the only wise God, through Jesus Christ, be the glory forever. Amen. (Romans 16:25-27)

Little children, guard yourselves from idols. (1Jn 5:21)